# THE WAY OF GRATITUDE

# THE WAY OF GRATITUDE

*A New Spirituality for Today*

Galen Guengerich

RANDOM HOUSE NEW YORK

Published in the United States by Random House,
an imprint and division of Penguin Random House LLC, New York.

RANDOM HOUSE and the HOUSE colophon are registered trademarks
of Penguin Random House LLC.

Permission credits can be found on page 219.

LIBRARY OF CONGRESS CATALOGING-IN-PUBLICATION DATA
Names: Guengerich, Galen.
Title: The way of gratitude: a new spirituality for today / Galen Guengerich.
Description: New York: Random House, 2020.
Identifiers: LCCN 2019045307 (print) | LCCN 2019045308 (ebook) |
ISBN 9780525511410 (hardcover) | ISBN 9780525511427 (ebook)
Subjects: LCSH: Gratitude. | Spiritual life. | Interpersonal relations.
Classification: LCC BJ1533.G8 G84 2020 (print) |
LCC BJ1533.G8 (ebook) | DDC 179/.9—dc23
LC record available at lccn.loc.gov/2019045307
LC ebook record available at lccn.loc.gov/2019045308

Printed in the United States of America on acid-free paper

randomhousebooks.com

9 8 7 6 5 4 3 2 1

First Edition

*Book design by Diane Hobbing*

*For Holly and Zoë*

In ordinary life we hardly realize that
we receive a great deal more than we give,
and that it is only with gratitude
that life becomes rich.

DIETRICH BONHOEFFER, 1906–1945

# CONTENTS

# PROLOGUE

THIS IS A book for spiritual seekers. Whether or not you have ever been part of a religious community, if you have ever sought a deeper sense of your life's meaning, a more compelling understanding of your life's purpose, or a more engaging experience of joy, then this book is for you.

Since I will be your guide along this journey of discovery, I begin in the first chapter by introducing myself and my own journey to you. As I often say, it has taken me "from Mennonite to Manhattan," both literally and metaphorically.

When I left the Conservative Mennonite Church in my late twenties, I had no idea that my newfound freedom would prove to be such a daunting challenge. To that point, I had mostly done what I was told—by my parents, by various church authorities, and ultimately by the dictates of the Bible. I didn't have to decide what to believe or how to live. My path had been signposted by someone else.

Once free from the constraints of my upbringing, I

began to realize that I was now in charge. I had to make my own signposts.

I had to decide how to live from day to day, a freedom I had long sought. But I also had to decide more fundamental things, such as what to believe and how to make sense of my life in terms of its larger purpose. How do I go about constructing a meaningful life? To what should my day-to-day activities add up over time? What about the big picture: How am I related to, and perhaps even responsible to, the people around me and the natural world? As I began to chart my own way, I wrestled with these questions.

Some years ago, on a visit to Israel, I spent some time with Natan Sharansky, a former Soviet chess prodigy who had spent time in prison because of his human rights activism. The Soviets eventually allowed Sharansky to emigrate to Israel, where he became involved in politics and continued his human rights work.

Sharansky told me that he learned the most important lesson of his life while in prison. People want two things, he said: They want to be free and they want to belong. But most people think freedom comes first and then belonging follows. What he realized in prison was that the opposite is true: You need to belong in order to be free. He illustrated his point by saying that you need to belong to a team in order to play in a soccer game, just as you need to belong to an orchestra in order to play a symphony. In the same way, he said, you need to be part of something—whether it's a family, a faith community, a people, a cause, or a country—in order to be free to make something of your life. In order for your life to have meaning and purpose, you need to belong.

This book is about my search for a new way to belong—not only to my own family of choice, which I eventually found, and not only to a new faith community, which I also eventually found, but to everything. Once I declared myself to be more a child of science than of scripture, and therefore more beholden to reason than to revelation, I needed a way to understand my life as meaningful in the modern world.

Part One of this book describes the human search for meaning—why it's important to us, how human beings have historically understood their lives as meaningful, and why so many of us face a crisis of meaning today. I explore the burgeoning interest in being spiritual but not religious, then focus on what I believe is the key to spirituality, which is the practice of openness. As we open ourselves, we begin to realize in a new way how much we rely on the people and world around us—and how much they rely on us. The appropriate spiritual response to this awareness, in my view, is gratitude, which I describe as our gateway to meaning. As we begin to develop gratitude as a way of life, we find ourselves experiencing not only a deeper sense of our life's meaning and purpose but also a more abiding sense of joy.

Part Two explores what I describe as the seven hallmarks of gratitude, which map our relationships to the people and world around us, and also describe our responsibilities in return. The way of gratitude is a journey toward increasing reciprocity with everyone and everything around us. The more aware we become of how much we rely on other people and on the natural world for everything that makes our lives possible and, if we are fortunate, sometimes wonderful, the more committed we become to making their lives better in return. I call these commitments "gratitude goals."

The final part of the book explores how we make the way of gratitude a practice—a spiritual practice. The only way we can be certain that the most important things in our life take precedence is to make them a regular part of our daily lives. In order to learn how to play the piano well, we need to practice the piano each day. The same is true of our spiritual lives. In order to develop a spiritual life that is meaningful, purposeful, and joyful, we need to undertake a way of life that makes these commitments an essential part of our daily lives.

As we make our way along this spiritual journey, I have included some poetry as an epigraph to each chapter. Why poetry? The purpose of poetry isn't merely to inform, or instruct, or explain, or even entertain. Its purpose is to inspire—inspire us to feel alive in a different way, inspire us to open ourselves to new experiences, inspire us to take risks. At its best, poetry distills an insight into a potent experience of transformation. Good poetry changes us.

Poetry has a special role to play when it comes to spirituality. It's my view that we need a touchstone to anchor our experience of grappling with the human desire to find a meaningful place for ourselves in the larger drama of time and history. Each of the established religious traditions of the West has its own scripture: the Torah of Judaism, the Bible of Christianity, the Quran of Islam. Likewise, one could say that the scripture of modern science is data, the touchstone of discovery and decision. For me, poetry is the scripture of contemporary spirituality—its touchstone. Poetry has long been an essential part of my own spiritual journey, and it's an essential part of this book. I encourage you to read the passages of poetry carefully and mull them over as you begin each chapter.

I hope that what I have found thus far on my journey through life will help you find your way too. And I'm eager for companions along the way. Come, let's take this journey together.

# THE WAY OF GRATITUDE

# Over the Edge

ॐ

What's madness but nobility of soul
At odds with circumstance? The day's on fire!
I know the purity of pure despair,
My shadow pinned against a sweating wall.
That place among the rocks—is it a cave,
Or winding path? The edge is what I have.

THEODORE ROETHKE (1908–1963),
EXCERPT FROM "IN A DARK TIME"

SOME YEARS AGO, my wife, Holly, and I made an overnight trip from Manhattan to Lancaster County, Pennsylvania. I had lived in the Lancaster area for a number of years beginning in my midteens, and eventually I had gone to college at Franklin & Marshall, where I majored in classics. Holly and I were on our way to attend a retirement party for the Latin professor who had chaired the classics department.

En route, as we meandered through lush Amish and Mennonite farms east of Lancaster, we passed a small Mennonite church out in the country. As we passed the church, Holly noticed that I had grown quiet, then pensive. "How do you feel about being here?" she asked. She knew that one of my uncles had once served that congregation as its pastor, and during my early twenties, I had been a youth minister there for a few years and then acting pastor for a short time. After a long pause, I replied, "Ambivalent. On the one hand, I feel claustrophobic—like I can't breathe. On the other hand, this is the mine where my gold came from."

When I was in my midtwenties, I left the Conservative Mennonite Church, the faith of my upbringing. It is the most difficult thing I have ever done.

Like their better-known Amish offshoots, the Conservative Mennonites of my childhood followed a simple and relatively austere way of life. We drove cars, but didn't watch television. We dressed plainly and unfashionably—two decades behind the times, not a century behind like the Amish, who don't use buttons, zippers, or synthetic fabrics. We attended church three times a week, singing hymns without musical accompaniment. The use of instruments might lead to dancing, which was "worldly" and therefore sinful. In that era, Conservative Mennonites didn't vote or otherwise become politically involved. In the language of the tradition, we were called to be "the quiet in the land," following the self-effacing example of Jesus in this life, even as we looked forward to extravagant rewards for our faithfulness in the next one.

Over the centuries, Mennonites developed their intentionally unobtrusive way of life because they often encountered withering persecution for their faith, especially for their steadfast commitment to pacifism and their belief that members should be baptized only as assenting adults, not as passive infants. This practice of baptizing people as adults, historically known as Anabaptism, was a capital crime (punishable by death) in parts of Europe during the late sixteenth and early seventeenth centuries. The Mennonites defended themselves against persecution by developing close-knit communities within cloistered environments. They kept quiet and kept to themselves. In the farming community where I grew up in central Delaware, virtually everyone was Mennonite—and many were related to me.

My father is a Mennonite minister, as was my maternal grandfather, along with seven of my eleven uncles and a dozen or so of my first cousins or their spouses. By the time I left the Mennonite church, I had spent several years in seminary preparing to be a Mennonite minister. When people ask me what I do for a living, I sometimes say that I'm in the family business. Except that I'm not.

Why did I leave? It wasn't because I took issue with people who strive to live simply and peacefully. Even today, as I look around at the many calamities in our world, I can confidently assert that the Mennonite way of life isn't part of the problem. If everyone lived simply and peacefully, the world would be a far better place.

I have also come to realize how much I gained from

my upbringing—the gold I took from the mine. I learned the importance of knowing what you believe. I learned how people in close-knit communities keep each other company in good times and support each other in difficult times. Especially during the years I lived on a farm, I learned the importance of hard work and perseverance. I also came to understand how completely we rely on the natural world, especially the plants and animals that provide us with sustenance. These experiences, and my reactions to them, have contributed decisively to my personal growth over the decades since.

Even so, my experience of growing up in a Mennonite cloister left me feeling trapped in a world that, for me at least, wasn't the real world. I felt like I was living someone else's idea of a life, based on a tradition of belief whose time had long passed. I wanted to be part of the world around me.

By the time I was in middle school, my family had moved to southern Arkansas, where my father started a Mennonite mission church. Though I attended public school, my parents tried to limit my exposure to the typical pursuits of teenagers at the time: watching television, listening to rock 'n' roll, going to the movies, and playing team sports, especially football. While I would eventually come to see the wisdom in some of my parents' limitations, I did not understand them at the time. I felt left out.

Ironically, my most painful experiences of being left out came when I ended up the focus of attention. Most of the time we were seated alphabetically in class. The girl who often sat behind me was, by general consensus, the prettiest girl in our class. In my view at least, she was also the nastiest. She happened to be captain of the cheerleading team. Predictably, her boyfriend was the quarterback of the football team. She delighted in tormenting me by acting in sexually suggestive ways toward me in front of her friends—including her boyfriend, the quarterback. I can still feel the humiliation.

As I gained my independence during my late teens and early twenties, I was gradually able to reduce the lifestyle differences between me and the non-Mennonites around me. Along the way, I became aware that these differences masked an underlying similarity. We shared many of our religious beliefs with the people around us—even the ones who lived differently. We as Mennonites were not alone in our loyalties.

Like many who practice one of the established religious traditions of the West (Judaism, Christianity, and Islam), Mennonites look to an ancient revelation as the source of their most trustworthy knowledge concerning what to believe and how to live. Scripture trumps science, and revelation trumps reason, when it comes to deciding the most important things in life. Also like many established traditions, Mennonites view this life mainly as a prelude to the next life—a "foretaste of glory divine," as a popular Mennonite hymn puts it. On these terms, *almost everything that has ultimate meaning either happened in the ancient past or will happen in the infinite future.*

I left the Mennonite church because I didn't want to live with my eyes closed and my mind made up. I wanted to open myself to discover meaning in what I learned from my own experience. I wanted to know joy in this life, not some future life.

It also became increasingly clear to me that I couldn't serve two masters if I ended up in the ministry: the biblically literalist doctrinal commitments of the church on the one hand (belief in a supernatural God, an inerrant scripture, the virgin birth, the resurrection, and so on) and the laws of nature as articulated by science and reason on the other. I couldn't preach one thing and believe another.

I also took personal issue with the view that, as the apostle Paul said in the book of Romans in the Christian New Testament, "All things work together for good to them that love God." Sometimes that may be true, but sometimes it's not. In 1996, my niece Krista died after an eight-year battle with a pernicious brain tumor. It was diagnosed when she was three years old, and she died when she was eleven. For nearly a decade, Krista's battle against the tumor defined our family life (and in many ways, it still does). Every year or so, we'd rendezvous for a week or more when Krista underwent brain surgery.

In the spring of 1996, my daughter, Zoë, and I went to my sister's home in the rugged hills of western Maryland to visit Krista one last time. Zoë was almost three years old at the time—the age Krista had been when the tumor was discovered. The three of us played endless games of "Crackers in My Bed." The game was simple enough for Zoë to understand, and the pieces were large enough that Krista could still see them if she sat under a bright light. After we'd played for a while, Krista would ask to be taken for one of her twice-daily naps. Zoë would help me push the wheelchair back to where a hospital bed had been set up in the bedroom. That's where Krista died several weeks later, a death that served no good purpose.

Though I had been gone from the Mennonite church for a decade by the time Krista died, her long saga of suffering and her tragically early death confirmed my reasons for leaving. All things work together for good? Not in this case.

When I left, I left everything behind—my marriage to a young Mennonite woman, my extended family, my church community, as well as the vocation for which I had prepared. Ripping myself out of the fabric of my life was painful beyond words, both for me and for the people I cared about, some of whom I hurt deeply, for which I am profoundly sorry. In the end, alone and on my own, I set out to find the way of life that was right for me.

Did I have doubts or second thoughts? Of course. As Theodore Roethke suggests in the title of his poem that opens this chapter, it was a dark time for me. In the opening line of the excerpt, Roethke gets the internal battle exactly right: "What's madness but nobility of soul / At odds with circumstance?" I felt there was a certain valor in my determination to chart my own course, but I found myself seriously at odds with the circumstances of my upbringing.

Many of my relatives thought my leaving was sheer madness, not to mention pure selfishness. They could never imagine doing what I was doing. Shortly after telling my extended family that I had decided to leave, I vividly recall opening my apartment door to find one of my older cousins, a Mennonite minister himself by then, who proceeded to try to talk me back from the precipice. He was the first of many who tried to convince me to stay.

I did feel a deep sense of loss at all I was leaving behind, but ultimately I felt I had no choice but to leave. The disparity between the Conservative Mennonite view of the world, which came from their idea of God, and my emerging view of the world, which came from human reason and experience, ultimately led me to "the edge," as Roethke put it.

The edge of what? Given that the original meaning of

the word "edge" referred to the blade of a knife, it suggests danger—the edge of a cliff, perhaps, or the brink of disaster. It also implies a border or a boundary—a place of transition, where you leave one community or culture and enter another. In my case, both meanings applied.

At the outset, despite the losses I had incurred, I found the experience of being on my own exhilarating, and also disorienting. Freedom, I came to learn, isn't initially a new sense of direction. Rather, it's the absence of something holding us back. As Janis Joplin sang, voicing Kris Kristofferson's haunting refrain, "Freedom's just another word for nothing left to lose."

As I made the transition from Mennonite to something else, I could easily have lost my way. For the first time in my life, I had no rules to follow, and no one would correct me if I went astray. I could do whatever I wanted during church times on Sunday morning, Sunday evening, and Wednesday evening. I could watch whatever I wanted on television—and even go to the movies. I could listen to whatever music I wanted—and even go dancing. Instead of living apart from the world, I became an active and engaged part of it.

By the time many young people leave home, they are happy to be gone from their parents' home. They are also often vehemently clear about the ways they don't want to be like their parents—the kind of neighborhood they don't want to live in, the kind of furniture they don't want to buy, the kind of food they don't want to eat. They soon learn, however, that the freedom to live anywhere you want doesn't mean you avoid eventually having to choose one particular place to call home. You have to furnish it with one particular assortment of furniture.

After I left the religious world of my upbringing, I faced a spiritual version of this dilemma. I no longer had to follow my parents' way of life. I could do whatever I wished. But I couldn't do everything. I had to choose a particular path for myself, based on commitments I decided to make and goals I chose to pursue. I found myself wondering what kind of a person I wanted to become and how I wanted to live. In order to be truly free, I eventually discovered, I needed to *belong* once again—but this time to a way of life that I had chosen for myself, *one that enabled me to find meaning and joy, here and now.*

My goal in this book is to articulate a new grounding for contemporary spirituality—one that will enable us to find meaning and joy in our daily lives, no matter our circumstances. I have developed this approach over nearly thirty years of ministry and now recommend it to you, whether you're a religious refugee or a spiritual seeker, or both. As with any path, the purpose is to develop a heightened sense of awareness that, over time, will lead to a more rewarding and joyful way of life. I can say with confidence that people who follow this path will gain a clearer sense of life's purpose and a fuller sense of its meaning.

If these experiences were easy to find, everyone would have already found them—and people like me wouldn't be writing books on the topic. But they are not easy to find, in part because spiritual experiences require radical openness, which can be hard to achieve. It may require us to make some changes in our priorities and our patterns of life. But what's better than feeling a deep sense of meaning and an abiding sense of joy?

If spirituality is the practice of opening ourselves to everyone and everything else, then gratitude is the leading indicator of our spiritual progress. Gratitude is the hallmark of people who practice radical openness to life. Its presence in our lives, moment by moment and day by day, becomes a source of meaning and joy that will not desert us, even in our most difficult times.

As the psalmist puts it, even in the midst of great distress, I am grateful that life has come my way. While the wisdom traditions of humanity differ in many ways, one thing they have in common is an emphasis on gratitude—the sign that we are engaging with life fully and completely. As we will see, modern science has come to the same conclusion: people who live with gratitude are happier and healthier than those who don't.

*

OVER THE PAST several decades, I've spent a significant amount of time in graduate school, studying theology and ethics. I have also become part of the Unitarian Universalist tradition, which departed from its Christian origins more than a century ago. For the past twenty-nine years, I have been a Unitarian Universalist minister, serving all but two of those years at All Souls in New York. Especially during the early years of my ministry, I most often encountered people like myself walking into the sanctuary. They, too, were refugees from one of the established religious traditions, looking for a new spiritual home.

Lucia Greenhouse, who with her husband and four children was part of my congregation for many years, tells about her crisis of faith in her memoir, *Fathermothergod: My Journey out of Christian Science*. Seven-year-old Lucia and her younger brother Sherman came home from school one day to find their older sister, Olivia, lying on the love seat, her exposed skin covered with red spots. Olivia announced that she had chicken pox, which Lucia attempted to confirm with her mother, who shushed her. "In Christian Science," her mother said gently, "we know that there is no illness. No disease. No contagion. Olivia is not sick. She is God's perfect child. We are all going to work very hard to keep our thoughts elevated."

Though Olivia recovered from her bout with chicken pox, Lucia's faith was deeply shaken by her mother's steadfast denial. A decade and a half later, when Lucia's mother fell ill with cancer, Lucia's faith reached a crisis point.

Torah Bontrager, another member of my congregation who found a new life after questioning the roots of her belief system, grew up Amish and fled after years of emotional and sexual abuse. She wrote, "At age 15, I escaped in the middle of the night without telling anyone goodbye. I left with only what I could carry: the clothes on my back and $170 USD in my pocket. My departure was permanent." Torah tells her story in *An Amish Girl in Manhattan: Escaping at Age 15, Breaking All the Rules, and Feeling Safe Again.*

In more recent years, people who enter All Souls for the first time increasingly have no firsthand experience of religious community. As countless newcomers from both backgrounds share their personal stories in my pastor's study, many describe themselves as spiritual but not religious. In so doing, they identify themselves as part of the fastest-growing religious cohort in the nation.

In my experience, this cohort of spiritually inquisitive seekers also includes people who participate in one of the established religious traditions because they value the sense of community and the collaborative approach to social justice, even though they don't necessarily subscribe to the doctrines and dogma. You may be one of those people. You may find many of the cultural forms of the tradition meaningful—the sense of belonging, perhaps the songs and stories, and maybe even some of the symbols and rituals—but you don't consider yourself a devout believer.

The idea that someone can be "culturally Jewish" is well known within the Jewish community, but there are many cultural Christians and cultural Muslims as well. In this sense, I consider myself a cultural Mennonite. The problem is that the cultural form of a tradition will only get you so far. It may last a generation or two. But free-floating forms of spirituality, whether they exist within an established tradition or beyond, ultimately need to find a new grounding based on what's deeply true about human life.

We find this new grounding, and we discover the experiences of meaning and joy that flow from it, when we shift our awareness from focusing mostly on ourselves as independent of other people and the world around us to focusing on how we are connected to everyone and everything else. Spiritual experiences move us beyond our own experiences here and now—what we need or want, maybe what we hope to get away with—to the awareness that we are inseparably part of a larger whole.

In the language of spirituality, this move to open ourselves to everything beyond ourselves is often described as the experience of transcendence. The word originally meant to pass over a physical obstacle, go beyond the limit, or climb over the top of a wall or mountain. In spiritual terms, transcendence is the ability to go beyond the confines of our daily lives and open ourselves to the reality of the larger world and our place in it. In its fullest sense, transcendence is the experience of opening ourselves wholly to everything.

Because we continually view the rest of the world only from the perspective of our individual lives, transcendence can be difficult to experience. The late American novelist David Foster Wallace told a parable that illustrates the reason why in his book *This Is Water,* which contains the text of a commencement address Wallace delivered to the graduating class at Kenyon College in 2005.

"There are these two young fish swimming along and they happen to meet an older fish swimming the other way, who nods at them and says, 'Morning, boys. How's the water?' And the two young fish swim on for a bit, and then eventually one of them looks over at the other and goes, 'What the hell is water?'"

The point of this story, Wallace explained, is that the most important realities are often the hardest to see. Each of us is like a fish in water: There is no experience we've had that we were not the absolute center of.

Transcendence is the process of trying to climb out of the water and see the reality of our lives and our relationship to everything else. In my way of describing spiritual experiences, they open us deeply and intimately to everything: all that is present in our lives and our world, as well as all that is past and all that is possible. These experiences expand our horizon of consciousness and open us fully to everyone and everything else. At their most fulsome, they are experiences of the divine.

## PART ONE

*Our Search for Meaning*

# Where Meaning Comes From

֍

if i can't have
what i want    then
my job is to want
what i've got
and be satisfied
that at least there
is something more
to want

NIKKI GIOVANNI (B. 1943), EXCERPT FROM
"CHOICES"

NIKKI GIOVANNI TITLED her poem "Choices," though
the poem is more about the choices she *doesn't* have
than those she does. Since she can't have what she
wants, go where she needs to go, or express what she
really feels, her job is to want what she already has, to
go where life points her, and to feel what she can express. The problem lies in the difference between the
first list and the second—between her aspirations and
the realities of her life. No matter our circumstances,
the reality of our lives rarely satisfies our aspirations.
Later in the poem, Giovanni concludes that human-

kind, alone among the animals, has for this reason learned to cry.

Giovanni wrote this poem as an African American woman, for whom the gap between aspirations and realities has produced great suffering and the shedding of tears. In a nation that has from the beginning privileged people who are male, white, and straight, the range of choices for people who don't check all these boxes, and especially for people who check none of them, has always been painfully limited and still is.

Despite this travesty, Giovanni acknowledges that she nonetheless has some choices in deciding how she lives. The same is true of everyone else—especially those of us who live in developed nations. Many of us enjoy a bewildering array of options for how to spend our days: what to learn, where to live, how to earn a living, what to do with our time, and with whom to develop emotional and physical relationships. We also face options in more trivial matters, such as which brand of coffee-maker to buy and whether to stay in for dinner or go out. Sometimes, the array borders on ridiculous.

My daughter, Zoë, once calculated how many restaurants would deliver to our home, which is located in an apartment building in Manhattan. She restricted her search to restaurants within one mile. Her answer came as a complete surprise to all of us: more than two hundred restaurants. Granted, more than two hundred thousand people live within a mile of our apartment.

But still, when it's dinnertime and everyone's hungry, it's hard to choose among twelve Mexican restaurants, twenty pizza restaurants, and thirty Chinese restaurants.

In restaurants, as in many other areas of life, while having some options is clearly better than having none, it's not clear that having many options is better than having a few. The process of choosing takes a considerable amount of time and energy. While options may at times seem boundless, time and energy are not.

Besides, no matter how many options we face in a given moment, we can choose only one of them, a reality check that's especially consequential with things that matter most in life, such as spouses, children, careers, or homes. There may be an opportunity to choose differently in the future, but once we have made our choice in the present, we can't unmake it. The more options you have, the better the chance you will end up choosing the wrong one—or at least one that's inferior to an option you didn't choose. Inevitably, some of our decisions will not turn out as we intended. For this reason, we need to understand the meaning of our lives in a way that doesn't depend on everything working out for good. Sometimes it doesn't.

THE PROBLEM OF having too many choices is, as they say, a first-world problem—or at least a modern-day problem. Most people throughout human history have had few options and thus few decisions to make. The necessities of nature dictated how they would live. The sole imperative of life was to survive. Find food and shelter. Bear children. Especially for our most distant predecessors, the struggle merely to stay alive dominated every moment of every day. This was their framework of meaning.

Over time, human beings figured out that certain choices about how to live were better than others. People who made bad decisions often weren't alive to repeat them. People who made good decisions—decisions that turned out to ensure safety, shelter, and sustenance—tended to make the same decisions over and over again. Most cultures eventually came to understand these successful patterns of living as mandatory rather than optional—derived not from the necessities of nature but from decrees that humans came to view as emanating from a divine source.

One key element in this transition emerged as a consequence of one of the best ideas humanity has ever had: the idea of agency. In this context, agency is the ability to make decisions and act on them within a given environment.

The process of natural selection gave preference to our predecessors who looked around and assumed that if something happened, someone or something *caused* it. If the reeds rustled at the water's edge, they figured out (probably the hard way) that they should see what was causing the rustle or they might become dinner. Sometimes, the action was driven by the instinct of an animal rather than by the decision of a human. Even so, the idea that things happen for a reason led our predecessors to conclude that since the world has been set in motion, someone or something must have caused that as well.

This insight led to the development of monotheism, the belief in the one true God. Thousands of years ago, inhabitants of the Ancient Near East (today's Middle East) developed the belief that God had set the world in motion and laid down rules for its inhabitants, whom God created in the beginning, along with the rest of the universe. In order to play this role, God would have to be supernatural—that is, exist in a realm that's above or beyond ("super") the natural world. (Ironically, this God turns out to be remarkably like human beings, except infinitely more knowledgeable and powerful. Instead of God creating human beings in the divine image, humans create God in their own image.)

Even though the three major monotheisms (Judaism, Christianity, and Islam) more or less agree that "God is one," they exhibit a remarkable variety of beliefs about almost everything else. They differ in their views of how God is one, which prophet most authoritatively speaks for God, what the faithful must believe, and how the faithful must live. Countless battles have been fought by humans wielding doctrines, swords, or both in order to prove the superiority of their form of belief or way of life.

Here's the basic reason for the variety: New ways of life develop when old ones aren't meaningful any longer, often because of conflict or oppression. For example, Judaism developed against a backdrop of the brutal centuries-long oppression of the ancient Semitic peoples by the Egyptians, according to the Hebrew Bible. Christianity developed as a protest against the way Jewish leaders had dealt with the ruthless occupation of the Jewish regions of Palestine by the Romans. Islam developed within the lengthy and destructive conflict between the monotheisms of Christianity and Judaism and the polytheisms of the ruling tribes in Arabia. In each case, a new voice eventually emerged from the turmoil: Moses, Jesus, and Mohammed, respectively. They diagnosed the problems of the day in spiritual terms and prescribed a new approach, one that would cast off the failed beliefs and practices of the past and usher in a new day of hope.

Each of these prophetic voices eventually expanded into a widespread movement. The initial insights developed into a tradition of interpretation, a pattern of spiritual practice, and a code of personal conduct. Other elements of a way of life emerged as well: songs to lift spirits in times of struggle, stories to recall the faithfulness of predecessors, symbols to remind them of their commitments, rituals to help bind them to each other and to God, and schools to educate their children and youth. Sometimes these elements were newly created, but often they were adapted from the culture and from existing religious traditions around them. Each way of life united its adherents within and distinguished them from others without. *Taken together, they formed a cohesive and comprehensive way of life, a durable expression of life's meaning and purpose.*

Inevitably, disagreements would appear within the new traditions. Sometimes these differences led to major divisions in the faith, such as between Sunni and Shia Islam in the seventh century or between Catholic and Protestant Christianity in the sixteenth century. Each of these new divisions would eventually divide again, and then again. Many of these newly formed ways of life flourished because they provided for their adherents a satisfying explanation of life's purpose, as well as a corresponding spiritual practice. They were able to infuse life with a sense of meaning and joy.

TODAY, AN ESTIMATED 84 percent of the people in the world adhere to one of humanity's countless religious traditions. More than half of the world's people—and more than three-quarters of the population in Western nations—follow one of the three monotheisms that trace their lineage back to the Hebrew patriarch Abraham: Judaism, Christianity, and Islam.

But especially in more recent times, many people have begun turning away from religion because they reject its underlying assumptions. In the modern world, the idea of a supernatural God can seem, well, farfetched—especially when some of the ancient beliefs and practices stand squarely at odds with what we now know to be true and beneficial. There are ways to understand the divine other than as supernatural, and I will explain my own understanding in due course. But when a tradition or congregation ignores the realities of the present out of loyalty to an outdated past, it can seem irrelevant to people who find life difficult or disconcerting, when the realities of their lives fail to align with their aspirations or when their choices are not satisfying.

I recall one young couple who first came to All Souls with their two children on the second Sunday after the terrorist attacks on the World Trade Center in September 2001. The first Sunday after the attacks they had gone to their usual house of worship and participated in a typical service there. The problem was that those were not typical days in New York City. The city had experienced a cataclysm of unprecedented proportions, and people flocked to houses of worship to find solace, as well as to be reassured that not everything had fallen down or fallen apart. In the case of this young couple, they received the same thing they had received in previous services, which had focused solely on the world of the Bible. As far as they could tell from the prayer, the sermon, and the other elements of the service, nothing unusual had happened in New York City five days before. Distressed by the lack of relevance, they left in search of meaning elsewhere, and a week later they ended up at All Souls.

Many Jewish, Christian, and Muslim congregations in the United States today have found ways to remain relevant to the modern search for meaning without cutting ties to their traditional commitments. But overall, the established religious traditions in the West have demonstrated an increasing lack of relevance (and in some cases, an increasing affliction of discrimination), which is why overall religious participation in the United States has declined precipitously over the past few decades, following a similar trend in Europe and the United Kingdom that extends back more than a century.

This decline has been fueled by the emergence of a historically new phenomenon in the West: a so-called secular way of life, one based on something other than belief in a supernatural God. The widespread and commonplace use of the word *secular* signals one of the most dramatic paradigm shifts in human history. Originally, the word referred to a period of time, such as a generation or an era. Early Christians used it to distinguish the eternal concerns of the church from the temporal preoccupations of the world outside the church—the secular. In more recent centuries, the word secular has come to describe a way of understanding existence, including human history, that doesn't require belief in God.

The catalyst for this shift was the rise of modern science, which began to change long-standing views of where our most certain knowledge as human beings comes from. Reason began to supplant divine revelation, and evidence began to take the place of divine decrees. For example, one way to read the creation story in the book of Genesis implies that the earth is a mere six thousand years old. But scientists have produced evidence—the decay of carbon in the earth's most ancient rocks—to prove conclusively that the earth is 750,000 times older than that.

This ability to choose whether or not to adopt a religious worldview lies at the heart of what secular means today. Ours is a secular age not because people today have stopped believing in God or participating in religious communities. Rather, people today have a choice about whether to view the world through the eyes of divine revelation or through the eyes of human reason. More and more people are choosing the secular option. *The question remains as to whether secular ways of life can also provide a satisfying source of meaning and joy.*

Many people, however, try to have it both ways—especially those of us who live in the West. We typically designate some parts of life "religious" and some parts "secular." Broadly speaking, people living in Western cultures usually designate politics, economics, and social matters as secular—in other words, everything public. The religious part of life is what remains: the personal encounter of the individual with the transcendent—the union of the one with the all, opening ourselves to everything beyond ourselves. This private experience is the principal domain of what we today more typically—and more accurately—call spirituality.

I recall a disturbing conversation I once had with a group of young adults from my congregation. My wife and I had invited them into our home for an evening of food and conversation. Since almost all of them had grown up elsewhere in the country, we talked about what had brought them to New York. Some had come for college or graduate school, while others had come in response to a job offer. Many had also come to escape something back home: a difficult family situation, a judgmental and bigoted community, or a dead-end vocational environment. We talked about what had drawn them to All Souls. Most had come seeking a sense of community. They were looking for a place of belonging in a hard-driving and often rough-and-tumble city.

Then I asked what they told their friends and colleagues at school and at work about All Souls—what it was like and why they participated. Their answer was unanimous: "We don't say anything," they said. "It's not acceptable among young people our age, at least in New York City, to be part of a religious community. Our friends would think we're deluded and crazy."

I realize that the situation would be reversed in some communities in the United States, where the expectation is that everyone goes to church—as indeed it was in the communities in the south when I grew up. Yet the trend is clear: More and more people view spirituality as something individuals can pay attention to if they wish. But it's not something that should be practiced collectively and certainly not in public.

It's my view that many people today have rightly recognized that established religions don't have all the answers, that some of the answers they offer don't make sense in our world today, and that some of the answers are downright destructive and offensive. *But the rise of interest in spirituality indicates that the longing for a comprehensive sense of meaning and a deep sense of purpose, a longing historically satisfied by religion, remains unmet by secularism.*

The modern-day divorce of the spiritual from the secular has turned out to be an often-unsatisfying exercise in existential schizophrenia. It separates the part of life that's supposed to inform our sense of meaning and purpose from everything else in our lives. Not that secularism can't provide people with a way of life, which it certainly can. But for many people today, secularism alone has turned out to be thin gruel in the meaning-of-life department.

ONE REASON FOR this lack of satisfaction may be the modern emphasis on the autonomy of the individual, a development that religion, ironically, helped precipitate. Five centuries ago, in 1517, a Christian monk named Martin Luther walked up to the door of the Castle Church in Wittenberg, Germany, and nailed a list of ninety-five revolutionary ideas to it—or at least that's the story as it's been handed down. More recently, historians have determined that Luther probably sent his document by mail.

His action sparked what came to be known as the Protestant Reformation, which divided the Western Christian church into two opposing, and often warring, factions: Protestants, who agreed with Luther, and Catholics, who did not. (I'm glossing over centuries of subtleties and divisions here, but these are the essential facts.)

Luther's primary claim in his declaration was that salvation is an individual matter, not an institutional one. To that point in the history of the Christian church, salvation was understood as coming to individual believers through the sacraments of communion and confession as administered by priests on the church's behalf. Luther drew a line straight from God to individual believers, cutting the church out of the process. On Luther's terms, confessing your sins directly to God brought immediate and full absolution directly from God.

Over the following centuries, the idea that individuals matter more than anything else caught on like wildfire. If you extend the primacy of the individual to politics, you get democracy. If you extend it to economics, you get free enterprise. Both focus on the individual—the desire of individuals to be self-governing and self-sustaining. In many other domains of life today, our roles are also self-determined, as a student, co-worker, parent, spouse, teammate, and so on. In each case, whether and how we fill these roles is largely a matter for us as individuals to decide.

For the most part, these have been exceedingly positive developments. Democratizing salvation has been a good thing. Democratizing the ballot box has been a good thing. Democratizing economics has been a good thing. In these and other arenas of human endeavor, the freedom of individuals to seek their own destiny has produced unprecedented levels of well-being and prosperity, especially in Western nations.

The shadow side of this development, however, has been the unwillingness of some individuals to see their own well-being as linked to the well-being of others. Individualism can easily turn selfish and narcissistic.

Democracy can be subverted when the few exert political control over the many. Free enterprise can be subverted when the few control most of society's economic capital. Religion has sometimes, though certainly not always, provided guardrails to constrain the worst excesses of individualism. Sometimes religion has exacerbated the problem. But especially in an environment where religion is in steep decline, the triumph of secularism gives as much reason to worry as to celebrate.

Here's why: On secularism's terms, when it comes to the meaning of life, we're each on our own. It's up to us to decide how the various domains of life fit together into a meaningful and satisfying whole, if indeed they do. Many people today who reject religion discover that secularism may have all the right pieces, or at least most of them, but it doesn't show us how the pieces fit together in a meaningful way. The disparate elements of our lives often don't cohere. The retreat of secularism into the autonomy of the individual turns out to be spiritually unsatisfying. Sequestered in this way, individuals are often unable to understand where they fit in—how the meaning of their lives connects to the people and world around them.

THIS RETREAT INTO the autonomy of the individual has also put our civic life as a nation at risk. As individuals, we understand our own lives mainly within the larger frameworks of meaning that we occupy. The decades-long decline of religion as one of those frameworks, while often justified, has had a troubling impact on our nation. Explaining why requires a look back at the founding of our nation.

The U.S. Declaration of Independence says that each of us has been divinely endowed with an unalienable right to "life, liberty, and the pursuit of happiness." If our happiness as individuals is the goal of life, the Declaration goes on to say, the question of what goals we should pursue as individuals is a matter for God to determine, not the state. Thus the question of how God intends us to live is a matter for each individual, or each religious community, to decide. With the European wars of religion still fresh in memory, the early architects of our political system were determined to keep the state out of these matters by protecting our freedom of conscience as individuals.

They came to this conclusion while making one key assumption. America was a nation of religious people, almost all of whom took the demands of their faith seriously. People went to church (or synagogue, though most of the early founders were Christian), where they supposedly learned about good and evil, right and wrong, and how to make choices that would create better lives for them and everyone else. The state's only concern was that one person's exercise of the freedom to pursue happiness did not impinge on the freedom of others. If it did, the state stepped in to ensure that the balance of liberty was set right.

Put differently, the state didn't need to concern itself with the creation of what I call moral capital—a sense of what constitutes a good life and an understanding of how to make morally coherent choices. That was the responsibility of individuals, and of families, and especially of houses of worship.

Given the steep decline in religious participation over recent decades, this source of moral capital has begun to dry up. Our public schools weren't designed to provide for the moral formation of our youngest citizens. Popular culture has become increasingly disdainful of any hint of moral discourse.

Increasingly, people in our nation and in other Western nations worship the idol of personal freedom, viewing happiness primarily as a form of private satisfaction. When freedom is understood in this narrow and self-serving way, happiness remains isolated from a source of value that links our individual happiness to the well-being of the people and world around us. As it turns out, this isn't just bad for us as individuals; it's bad for the character of our nation.

I recall a scene from Jonathan Franzen's novel *Freedom,* which tells the story of Walter and Patty Berglund, a couple from Saint Paul, Minnesota. Late in the book, we encounter a telling conversation between Walter and his brother Mitch, an alcoholic ne'er-do-well who has fathered five children with three different women and subsequently abandoned all of them. Walter had lost track of his brother, but eventually discovers him living a hardscrabble existence in the woods of Minnesota and pays him a visit. Walter asks Mitch whether he has enough money.

Mitch leaned over somewhat unsteadily and opened a tackle box in which there was a small pile of paper money and maybe fifty dollars in coins. "My bank," he said. "I got enough to last through the warm weather. I had a night-watchman job in Aitkin last winter."

"And what are you going to do when this runs out?"

"I'll find something. I take pretty good care of myself."

"You worry about your kids?"

"Yeah, I worry, sometimes. But they've got good mothers that know how to take care of them. I'm no help at that. I finally figured that out. I'm only good at taking care of me."

"You're a free man."

"That I am."

Mitch is the purest American in the book: He believes freedom is about, as he says, "taking care of me." To the extent that I as an individual believe freedom is solely about taking care of myself, I'm doomed, as are those around me who depend on me.

As I stated earlier, I believe the rise of secularism and the corresponding decline of religion are largely positive developments. But this dramatic shift has left many individuals without a clear source of spiritual meaning and our nation without a clear source of collective moral purpose. Here's the question that remains: Can we discover a way of life that enables us fully to accept modern views of knowledge, yet grounds our spirituality in a way that satisfies our individual quests for meaning and joy, and also provides a framework for understanding our responsibilities as citizens? To answer this question, we turn first to the practice of openness, and then to the experience of gratitude.

# CHAPTER 3

# How We Open Ourselves
## to Meaning

ॐ

People will tell you there are many good lives
Waiting for everyone, each fine in its own way.
And maybe they're right, but in my opinion
One is miles above the others.
Otherwise it wouldn't have been so clear to me
When I found it. Otherwise those who lack it
Wouldn't be able to tell so clearly it's missing
As they go on living as best they can
Without complaining. Noble lives, and beautiful,
And happy as much as doing well can make them.
But as for the happiness that can't be earned,
The kind it makes no sense for you to look for,
That's something different.

CARL DENNIS (B. 1939), EXCERPT FROM
"AUNT CELIA, 1961"

IF SPIRITUALITY IS the practice of openness, then I was
brought up to be one of the least spiritual people on the
planet. Growing up Mennonite was, at least for me, an
experience of being closed off to other people and the
world around me. In retrospect, it seems like the spiri-

tual discipline we were expected to practice involved denying that there was anything attractive about other ways of life.

Even so, the work of opening myself to the world beyond my own experience began early. Perhaps because we didn't have a television, I became a voracious reader, as did my younger sister and brother. Beginning in middle school, my family made weekly treks to the public library in town. I would return home each time with a dozen or more books. A few years later, the library named our family "Library Family of the Year," an honor that included an article in the local newspaper, complete with a photo of us surrounded by our stacks of library books, reading. Neither the article nor the photo of me—with an uneven haircut and woefully unstylish clothes—did anything to improve my renown at school.

But the books began to open my world. I learned about airplanes and imagined myself flying fighter planes in the Air Force. I learned about traveling to outer space (this was the era of the Apollo moon landings) and imagined myself blasting out of Earth's orbit as an astronaut. I imagined myself as beset by adventure as the Hardy boys and as plucky and courageous as Nancy Drew. Ron Koertge whimsically expresses Nancy's resourcefulness in his poem "Nancy Drew," when he says: "Locked in the pantry of an abandoned farm house, / Nancy makes a radio out of a shoelace and a muffin. / Pretty soon the police show up, and everything's / hunky dory."

Of course, it's one thing to open our minds to learn something about the world around us, or to even imagine ourselves in a different time and place, but it's quite another to open our hearts to the experiences of other people, especially when they are feeling pain—and even more especially when we have caused that pain. As we will discover, sometimes it takes an emotional cataclysm to get through to us.

IN THE POEM "Aunt Celia, 1961" by Carl Dennis, Aunt Celia decides to travel to Pittsburgh to visit her cousin in the spring of 1930. Aunt Celia was going through life alone and had mostly given up thinking she could find a man who suited her. But then her cousin invited her to Pittsburgh, and she decided to accept the invitation.

While there, her cousin brought her to a lecture at the local socialist club. After the talk, Aunt Celia forgot her scarf, but decided to go back and get it. That's when she discovered the cheerful and philosophical man who eventually became Uncle Harry.

But, Aunt Celia wondered several decades later, what if she had declined the invitation to Pittsburgh or postponed the trip by a week to be home for her mother's birthday? What if she had decided not to go back and get her scarf? The poem ends with the lines excerpted at the beginning of this chapter.

Most people, the poem notes, think there are many good ways of living waiting for everyone, and each way of living is fine in its own way. Well lived, each life can be noble and beautiful, even happy. Anyone who ends up living such a life would have nothing to complain about.

But, the poem concludes, there's another kind of life altogether, one that makes no sense even to look for. It ushers in a kind of happiness that can't be earned. This kind of happiness is "something different."

The practice of openness invites the kind of happiness that can't be earned—the kind it makes no sense to look for precisely because we don't know exactly what we are looking for, or why. We want the kind of meaning that can't be found under a microscope, the kind of purpose that can't be derived by a proof, the kind of satisfaction that can't be achieved by reaching even the most distant goal, the kind of joy that can't be identified by an algorithm. We want to put ourselves where we can be found by the joy of discovering who we are, where we belong, and what the days of our lives ultimately mean.

On these terms, spirituality isn't the experience of looking for happiness. Rather, it's what Walt Whitman, in his poem "Song of the Open Road," calls "the profound lesson of reception." It is the practice of radical openness to life, of exposing ourselves not just to some things but to everything. It's the desire to dig deep, as Ralph Waldo Emerson says. It's the desire to take the world into our arms, as the poet Mary Oliver says. Spirituality is marked by curiosity—by awareness that there is more to the picture than we are seeing, more to the situation than we currently know about, more to the person than what we've already noticed. Spirituality invites us to live with all our senses, taking it all in. There's always more.

Spirituality is the deliberate commitment to a world of experience that we know nothing about—and will continue to know nothing about unless we practice being available and becoming aware. The opposite of openness is a spiritual form of narcissism, which is the default mode of living, especially in the West. Our culture focuses relentlessly on the individual: what *I* think, what *I* feel, what *I* know, what *I* want, what *I* need. This approach lives in ignorance of everyone and everything else. In this case, ignorance is not bliss; ignorance is simply ignorance—not knowing what there is to know, not seeing what there is to see, not experiencing what there is to experience.

Spiritual practice is so called for a reason: It takes practice, it takes patience, and it takes persistence.

\*

SPIRITUALITY OPERATES IN the domain of experience. The practice begins by acknowledging the closed-off areas of our lives, and it progresses by intentional and repeated efforts to open them up—a process to which we shall return in Part Three of the book.

If facts are musical notes on a page, then spirituality is the music they create. For my part, I knew a lot of notes, but I wasn't very good at listening to the music.

You might call my upbringing a perfect storm of emotional denial. For the most part, growing up Mennonite involved denying we even *had* emotions, much less that we should express them. The Mennonite tradition bequeathed to me and my family of origin the conviction that emotions could easily run afoul of God's will. If you felt too happy, you might begin to take credit for your happiness, which rightly belongs to God. Too much happiness might lead to dancing, which would be even worse. This has become a punch line between my wife, Holly, and me when we're having a good time: This could lead to dancing. On the other hand, if you felt too sad, my Mennonite upbringing suggested, you would thereby deny God's perfect will, which supposedly ensures that everything works out for good.

In addition, or perhaps as a result, I grew up in a family that I would describe as emotionally reticent. I don't recall my father ever talking about his feelings. In fact, I remember many instances when he reacted negatively to other people expressing their feelings. It was almost a sin to have emotions because they indicated your narcissism.

I also grew up as a straight white male in a culture that privileges straight white males. There were lots of things that I didn't have to wonder about, worry about, or fear. There were also lots of things that I didn't have to feel especially good about, happy about, or relieved about. The way things were didn't provoke feelings of any sort, because they were, well, just the way things were—at least for a straight white male.

Because of my upbringing, I have long had a built-in tendency to be less emotionally aware and expressive than I would like. Sometimes people interpret my emotional reticence as aloofness or even intellectual arrogance. These are understandable mistakes on their part, but they are mistakes nonetheless. Admittedly, the demands of my professional life exacerbate this problem. My focus as a minister typically lies on the needs of the people around me and their challenges of living in the world we share. My own feelings have always seemed beside the point.

As an adult, my ongoing task has been to develop my emotional intelligence. Like any other language, the language of feelings is much harder to develop during adulthood than it is to learn during childhood. When it comes to acknowledging my feelings and expressing them, I'm still a work in progress. My wife, Holly, has been my steadfast mentor in this endeavor. She's one of the most emotionally intelligent people I know, and I'm deeply grateful for her patience over the years.

In addition to being closed off by patterns we may develop early in life, we can also find ourselves closed off by ways of living we develop as adults. Make no mistake: These patterns don't necessarily conform to what we like or even what we want. Some decisions are forced on us by circumstances, other people, or prior decisions we have made. But regardless of whether or not we like the ways of living that constitute our lives, the patterns themselves prove remarkably durable, both for better and for worse.

As these patterns accrue over time, they increasingly define who we are and how we relate to the people and world around us. Taken together, they constitute a way of life. It may not be the way of life we hope for or aspire to, but it's ours, shaped by choices and commitments we have already made.

As we develop more fully our individual way of life, we inevitably close ourselves off to other paths. We don't start with a blank slate each morning. We know which home is ours, which clothes are ours, which job is ours, and which children are ours. We know which bills we have to pay, which meetings we have to attend, and which hours are available for sleep. We may need to pay attention to each individual commitment as we fulfill it, whether paying the rent or showing up at work.

We may decide in what order things get done. But we don't need to make many decisions about what's on our to-do list. We just do what's required of us. We do the next thing. And the next thing.

This tendency to live our lives on autopilot has been exacerbated in recent years by our increasing fixation with digital media—by the screen that's in front of us, which closes us off in a different way. We don't need to figure out how to get somewhere because our smartphones can tell us. We don't need to talk to the people around us when we're waiting in line at the grocery store because we can check our email or watch a video.

The current generation of high school students—Generation Z, as some call them, or the iGeneration—grew up with smartphones. They don't remember a time before the Internet. As intensive consumers of technology and adroit multitaskers, they are more connected digitally than any previous generation, but they also tend to be more isolated personally. Rates of loneliness, depression, and suicide among teens have skyrocketed in recent years, a trend some recent research has linked to the rise in use of smartphones and social media. The rise in unhappiness among teens tracks almost exactly the rise in screen time.

At the level of life's most daunting challenges, the smartphone turns out to be an instrument not of connection, but of isolation. If a smartphone is the principal means by which teens end up relating to other people, it ultimately leaves them on their own to find their way in the world. Over time, these patterns of isolation will apply to everyone. Ironically, the technology that opens the world to us ends up closing us off from the things that matter most.

YET NO MATTER how barricaded our lives become, something will inevitably break through—and it's usually traumatic: a nasty accident, a grim diagnosis, the sudden death of someone we love, a cataclysmic failure in love, or an unwelcome transition at work. Someone who has been steadily present in our lives, or some capability or role that has helped define our existence, has been called into question or taken from us.

I recall one of those cataclysms unfolding at dinner on a late fall evening when Zoë was in her midteens. The conversation among the three of us had drifted into an area of our family life that had become particularly fraught over the preceding weeks. The exact nature of the issue is less important than the fact that it was a situation in which I, as Zoë's father, needed to take the lead in addressing the issue with her, rather than waiting until Holly, Zoë's stepmother, became exasperated enough with the situation to bring it up herself. Wishing to avoid the inevitable conflict (recall that Mennonites are pacifist, in more ways than one), I had put it off. The ensuing conversation, which was high decibel and hugely devastating to all of us, ended with Zoë sobbing in the hallway outside our apartment, Holly fuming in her study, and me sitting at the dining room table, wondering what exactly had happened.

As the three of us began to put the pieces back together over the next few days and weeks, I came to realize in a new way that my long-standing experience of openness to the facts about the world around me needed to expand to include my openness to the feelings of the people around me—to their experience of me and of everyone and everything else.

I also realized that I needed to open myself to the way things actually are—not the way I wished they were, the way I thought they should be, or the way I hoped they would turn out. When it came to the most important things in my life, and especially the most important people in my life, what I didn't know could end up hurting me, not to mention hurting the people I care about deeply. Almost always, choosing to know is better than choosing not to know.

Sometimes what breaks through, however, is far beyond our control. Our way of life may be brutally interrupted, maybe even torn apart.

For many of us in the United States, the morning of September 11, 2001, was one of those moments of reckoning. Perhaps especially for those of us who were living in New York City at the time, the terrorist attacks on the Twin Towers of the World Trade Center obliterated the ways of life that we had long taken for granted. The New York City skyline looked profoundly different in the aftermath, as did almost every other aspect of life.

On that fateful morning, which was a primary election day in New York City, a woman named Hilary North decided to stop on her way to work in order to vote. As a result, she was late getting to her office on the 103rd floor of the South Tower of the World Trade Center. If she had arrived on time, she almost certainly would have died, along with 176 of her co-workers.

Shortly after 9/11, North sat down and made a list of the ways her life had changed as a result of the attacks. Her list, titled "How My Life Has Changed," includes the following:

> I can no longer flirt with Lou.
> I can no longer dance with Mayra.
> I can no longer eat brownies with Suzanne Y.
> I can no longer meet the deadline with Mark.
> I can no longer talk to George about his daughter.
> I can no longer drink coffee with Rich.
> I can no longer make a good impression on Chris.
> I can no longer smile at Paul.
> I can no longer confide in Lisa.

She ends her list:

> I can no longer say hello to Steven every morning.
> I can no longer see the incredible view from the
>     103rd Floor of the South Tower.
> I can no longer take my life for granted.

When something breaks through the patterns that shield us and the routines that insulate us, we have an opportunity to start paying attention to things we have long taken for granted. We have a chance to open our minds and our hearts to a universe of experience that we have been missing. More than anything else, this presents us with a spiritual challenge.

SEVERAL YEARS AGO, I participated in a conference on spirituality and sustainable agriculture at Harvard Divinity School. One of the speakers was a young woman named Sarah Williams, who was completing a degree in sustainable agriculture at Evergreen State College in Olympia, Washington. She described a practicum she took during her second semester at Evergreen.

As I recall the story, she was assigned to a farmer in the area, one who practiced biodynamic farming and also happened to be Native American. When she showed up at the farm for the first time, the farmer greeted her and then led her to a large tree standing on its own somewhat away from the farm buildings.

"Your work this semester," the farmer told her, "is to sit with this tree."

She was dumbfounded. "But what am I supposed to do?"

The farmer replied, "You are supposed to sit with the tree."

"What does that mean?" she asked.

"The tree will tell you what that means."

For several hours each week for the rest of the semester, Sarah Williams sat with her tree. Since she began in January, there wasn't much to see at first, at least to her eye. Against the sky, the sturdy trunk stood tall and silent, the bare branches occasionally swaying in the breeze and sometimes whipping in the wind. When it rained, she watched the water run down the bark and into the ground.

As she watched the water disappear, however, she realized that she could only see half of her tree—maybe even less than half. Its roots plunged deep into the earth below, holding tight against the wind and drawing water and nutrients from the soil and sending them upward into the trunk and out to the branches.

When spring came, she watched buds form on the branches and the leaves unfurl. She already knew about photosynthesis, the work of leaves, which transform sunlight and water into carbohydrate molecules, providing fuel for the rest of the tree's work. From the perspective of a leaf, the oxygen it gives off is merely a waste product.

Week after week, Sarah Williams sat with her tree. She saw bugs appear on the bark, and birds show up to feed on them. She saw worms aerating and enriching the soil beneath the canopy—and birds feeding on the worms. Over time, she began to realize what the farmer wanted her to understand. Her tree was alive. While she could have said beforehand that all trees are alive, she had never realized how fully alive each tree was—and how much a community of life it was. Each leaf and branch on her tree was alive, as was each individual bug, and each individual bird, and each individual worm. Her tree was a community of life—alive in its own unique, distinctive, and irreplaceable way.

Sarah Williams only noticed these things because she paid careful attention over a long period of time. She practiced the discipline of openness. In much the same way, we need to develop the practice of opening ourselves to the people and world around us—the discipline of *paying attention*. What we will discover is that the outer limit of our attention can extend much further than we initially might think.

In recent decades, physicists working at the forefront of human knowledge have attempted to reconcile Einstein's theory of relativity and its explanation of large interactions (among gravity, light, planets, and so on) with quantum mechanics and its explanation of small interactions (among photons, neutrinos, quarks, and the like). String theory, as this unified explanation has come to be known, suggests that, in addition to the four dimensions of space and time that we already know about (length, breadth, depth, and time), the universe may also contain up to seven other dimensions that we haven't discovered yet.

This field of inquiry confirms what many human beings have always believed: The known universe reveals only part of the story of the cosmos. Hindus believe the soul survives death to be reincarnated into a new physical body, a cycle that continually repeats itself. Christians believe the soul survives death to exist eternally either in heaven or in hell. Spiritualists believe the souls of the dead have the ability to communicate with the living and provide them with spiritual guidance.

I'm not suggesting that string theory validates any of these claims, but I am saying that we should approach the question of what we know to be true or not true, and especially of what we know to exist or not exist, with a profound sense of humility. From a cosmic perspective, our ignorance is vastly more complete than our knowledge. In many contexts, we don't even know what we don't know. The only reasonable response to this conundrum is to practice the spiritual discipline of radical openness—to take in everything we can.

People who are committed to a spiritual approach to living are committed to finding out the truth about everything—the amazing things about people and the world around us, and also the difficult things. Some of what there is to know about other people and about the world is unpleasant, even horrific—life's "genuine meanness," as Emerson says.

But living in ignorance of what's true about the people and world around us doesn't make us happier; it ultimately makes us more fearful. In some cases, if what there is to know about other people or the world around us is a hard truth, we can work to make things better. In others, we can defend ourselves and those we love against the horrors of the world. Because spiritual people know there's always more, we live with optimism— the knowledge that something better is possible. As the scripture says, truth will set you free.

# CHAPTER 4

# Gratitude: Our Gateway to Meaning

No other word will do. For that's what it was. Gravy.
Gravy, these past ten years.
Alive, sober, working, loving and
being loved by a good woman. Eleven years
ago he was told he had six months to live
at the rate he was going. And he was going
nowhere but down. So he changed his ways
somehow. He quit drinking! And the rest?
After that it was *all* gravy . . .

RAYMOND CARVER (1938–1988),
EXCERPT FROM "GRAVY"

I WAS A chubby child growing up, no doubt due partly to nature and partly to nurture. The austere Mennonite culture of my upbringing admitted relatively few pleasures, but one happy exception was food, which our farms and gardens supplied in abundance. As a result, I wasn't the only one who was chubby. Besides, I had developed a fondness for my maternal grandmother's homemade bread, which she made fresh every day, amply slathered with her homemade butter and strawberry jam. I also inherited my father's fondness for pie.

When I entered my teens, however, I began to lose weight, which seemed like a good thing to me and everyone else. As my weight decreased, my energy level increased. At least at the outset, adolescence appeared to be smiling on me.

When I turned fourteen, I decided that I wanted to work part-time at the county-owned nursing home with which our church was affiliated. In order to qualify, I needed a work permit, which required securing a medical clearance. My mother took me to our family physician, who conducted the required tests and filled out the necessary paperwork. With our mission accomplished, my mother and I headed for the door.

As we reached the far end of the waiting room, the doctor reappeared in his office door and called out to me. "I just want to check one more thing," he said. He asked me to hold out my hands, which I did. He noticed a slight tremor. "I'd like to run one more blood test," he said, "just to be on the safe side."

Two days later, I found myself in the hospital being prepped for surgery to remove a toxic thyroid (an exceedingly rare condition in young people, especially young males), which had caused my weight loss. As it turned out, the surgeon wouldn't decide it was safe to operate for about six weeks, given the high risk of a fatal heart attack. Although everything eventually turned out all right, it's almost certain that I would have died of a heart attack if our family physician hadn't paid attention to his instinct that something wasn't quite right. But I didn't die, which is something of a marvel.

More than that, I was alive in the first place, which is even more of a marvel. In Bill Bryson's book *A Short History of Nearly Everything,* he notes that everything is made of atoms, which are rather small (five hundred thousand lined up shoulder to shoulder could hide behind a human hair) and rather plentiful (air the size of a sugar cube contains about forty-five billion billion molecules, each made of two or more atoms). Atoms are also virtually indestructible, which is why they constantly get recycled by the great wheel of life. Yet, Bryson says, trillions of these atoms have somehow assembled themselves into you—an arrangement so specialized and particular that it has never been tried before and will exist only this once.

He adds, "It is a slightly arresting notion that if you were to pick yourself apart with tweezers, one atom at a time, you would produce a mound of fine atomic dust, none of which had ever been alive but all of which had once been you. Yet somehow for the period of your existence they will answer to a single rigid impulse: to keep you you."

No one knows from where this impulse comes. The force that calls trillions of atoms to assemble into a living human being and stay that way for the better part of a century is as mysterious and marvelous as anything

I know. Even in the face of death, but perhaps especially then, it's a gift beyond measure to be alive when you stop to think about it. Gratitude seems like the only possible response to the gift of another day.

The experience of gratitude offers ample rewards—to our minds as well as our bodies, and to ourselves as well as to everyone and everything around us. I embrace gratitude as the fundamental way of relating to everyone and everything else not only because it's useful, but because it correctly describes the nature of those relationships.

Gratitude has its basis in our awareness of all the things that have come our way from the people and world around us. We begin with this inescapable reality: We are contingent creatures. We depend on our environment for everything we need. We depend on the largess of the natural world for our very existence, and we depend on the people around us for the quality of our ongoing lives. Without the natural world, we wouldn't have air to breathe, water to drink, or food to eat. Without biological parents to conceive us, none of us would have been born. Without nurturing hands to care for us during our infancy, none of us would have survived. Without people around to teach us how to use language and how to accomplish the basic tasks of daily human life, none of us would be able to fend for ourselves. And without the institutions of human civilization, such as schools and hospitals, not to mention governments, none of us would be able to realize our potential as human beings.

Gratitude is a way of life that, when consistently practiced, leads to an abiding sense of joy—joy at being alive, joy at being part of this amazing ecosystem we call planet Earth, joy at being able to begin each morning with the gift of a new day, joy at being able to love and work, and sometimes struggle and occasionally fail, and then begin again.

The poet Raymond Carver died of cancer eleven years after he was told he had only six months to live because of his alcoholism. Confronted by the hard truth about his alcoholism and his impending death, Carver responded by transforming his life completely. "Gravy," the poem that begins this chapter, was one of the last poems he wrote before he died.

What Carver called gravy, I call gratitude—an acknowledgment of what we have been given, as well as what we owe back in return. By gravy, I don't take Carver to be talking only about the good stuff on top of all the other stuff (a southern friend from my youth used to speak of "the icing on the gravy"). Rather, as Carver wrote, it's all gravy—all of it.

Or as I prefer to say, it's all gratitude. The good stuff, the bad stuff, the easy stuff, the hard stuff: all gratitude. It's a gift worth discovering—one I invite you to explore with me more fully when we examine the hallmarks and then the practice of gratitude.

\*

"COUNT YOUR MANY blessings, name them one by one," instructed the refrain of one of the hymns we frequently sang in church when I was young. The call to identify our blessings by name and express gratitude for them resounds consistently throughout the religious traditions of humanity.

Indeed, the Hebrew term for gratitude is *hakarat hatov,* which means "recognizing the good." Practicing gratitude means recognizing what's good in your life, even if there are bad things you could name as well. If you've been laid off from your job, but you're healthy and able to work, you can be grateful for that. If the power goes out in a storm, but your home keeps out the wind and the rain, you can be grateful for that. If your physical vitality has been declining, but your mind remains keen, you can be grateful for that. As the first century rabbi Simeon ben Zoma famously put it, "Who is rich? Those who are happy with what they have."

The Christian New Testament counsels the same approach to life. In one of his letters, the apostle Paul instructed believers to give thanks "at all times and for everything." In another, he said they should "rejoice always, pray without ceasing, and give thanks in all circumstances." The Quran echoes this admonition: "Those who are grateful do so to the profit of their own souls." Practicing Muslims begin their morning prayers with an expression of gratitude and thanksgiving.

Jews, Christians, and Muslims tend to direct their gratitude toward God, whom they believe is responsible for all the blessings they enjoy. I find this level of divine responsibility difficult to accept. If God is directly responsible for all the good things I enjoy, then God must also be directly responsible when other people, equally deserving, don't enjoy those same good things. In addition, God would need to answer not only for the absence of good things, but also for the presence of bad things—unless one invokes an almost-as-powerful malicious presence in the world, such as Satan. However, I don't see any evidence that this is a divinely and satanically commanded and controlled universe.

But that doesn't mean we shouldn't be grateful for the good things that come our way. From whatever source, the good things we enjoy are genuinely good, and they are well worth being grateful for.

WE RARELY STOP to think about our good fortune at being alive, unless life prompts us to do so. My experience over several decades of ministry has been that most people who look death full in the face and live to tell about it find themselves profoundly changed by the experience. Once you know that you're lucky to be alive, you feel, well, lucky to be alive. Even if nothing ulti-mately changes, everything's different. Flowers appear more vivid, lemons taste more pungent, and music sounds more enthralling. Each day dawns as an over-ture and departs as an encore.

Some people respond with gratitude for what they have been given even when death is close at hand. Some years ago, I made a hospital visit to a woman I'll call Marika, who was terminally ill with a relatively rare and extremely persistent cancer. She had come to this country from Malaysia before her then-twelve-year-old daughter, whom I'll call Aisha, was born. Marika had raised Aisha as a single parent, without benefit of ex-tended family. The two of them had been attending All Souls for about a year.

Marika and I talked about the challenges she had faced in her life, and especially her frustration that her cancer had not been diagnosed earlier. But mostly, we talked about Aisha—about the arrangements Marika had made for her to remain in this country and the hopes she had for her as a young woman.

Then Aisha walked into the room from one of her first days in school. I liked her immediately. She was an energetic and confident young woman. We talked about the courses she was taking and her new teachers—which ones were on the most sought-after list and which ones were not. Marika listened without com-ment, smiling with obvious pride, yet wistful at knowing her time with Aisha was soon to end. Then Aisha headed down to the cafeteria for an after-school snack.

Marika and I sat in silence for a few moments, and then she said, "I'm so grateful that Aisha has been able to grow up in this country." She paused, and then added, "I'm even more grateful that I have had twelve wonderful years with her."

This heartfelt response stopped me short—especially since Aisha was about the same age as my daughter, Zoë. Given Marika's looming far-too-early death, she had every right to be angry, bitter, and overwhelmed with sorrow, but she wasn't. She somehow kept her focus on the good things that remained in her life, not on the future that she had lost. For her, what remained was blessing enough.

This sense of gratitude for what we have emerges most forcefully when we face the prospect of losing it. But the key to living with a deep and abiding sense of joy is to develop the practice of gratitude before experiences of loss come our way.

RABBI BEN ZOMA was right: People who are happy with what they have turn out to be wealthy in every sense that matters. And while our bank accounts may not grow when we express our gratitude for what we have, the Quran is right that our souls profit when we name our blessings.

Our minds and bodies profit as well. Extensive research has shown that people who cultivate gratitude are physically healthier and emotionally happier than people who don't. Grateful people have fewer aches and pains, sleep better, and find it easier to develop relationships with other people. They are happier, more sensitive and empathetic, and more resilient. They have a better sense of self-esteem.

That's not to say that we always need to *feel* grateful. In his book *Gratitude Works!: A 21-Day Program for Creating Emotional Prosperity*, Robert Emmons draws an important distinction between feeling grateful and being grateful. He writes, "We don't have much control over our emotions. We cannot easily will ourselves to feel grateful, to feel less depressed, or to feel happy." He goes on to say that our feelings follow from the way we look at the world—from the distance between our thoughts about the way things are and our thoughts about the way things should be. "But being grateful is a choice," he says, "a prevailing attitude that endures and is relatively immune to the gains and losses that flow in and out of our lives."

This distinction between feeling grateful and being grateful is important to keep in mind. If we only express gratitude when we happen to be feeling grateful, we will lose the benefit. The purpose of making gratitude a practice is not only to create spaces in our lives for experiences we value, but also to maintain places in our lives for those experiences when they're missing.

Gratitude is the practice of radical openness to whatever comes our way, whether for good or for ill. It's a way of living that understands the meaning of our lives in terms of our relationships to the people and world around us. The practice of gratitude enables us not only to embrace the good experiences in our lives, but also to endure the difficult experiences and seek to transform them. It points the way from what is present to what is possible.

If we are fortunate, the people and world around us have given us what we need to develop physical and emotional maturity. We become spiritually mature as we realize what we owe in return. Whenever our vast array of relationships includes experiences of pain or even perversity, life invites us to be grateful for what we have been given and to be agents of healing and hope. When these relationships are beneficial and beautiful, we find ourselves experiencing what Carl Dennis called "the happiness that can't be earned." The spiritual term for this kind of happiness, in my view, is joy.

# CHAPTER 5

# Joy: Our Reward for Gratitude

ॐ

Joy, in Nature's wide dominion,
Mightiest cause of all is found;
And 'tis joy that moves the pinion,
When the wheel of time goes round.

FRIEDRICH SCHILLER (1759–1805),
EXCERPT FROM "ODE TO JOY"

IN THE SUMMER of 2005, my wife, Holly, my daughter, Zoë, and I took a once-in-a-lifetime, dream-come-true vacation: a weeklong horseback ride through the Loire Valley in France. I was a completely inexperienced rider, which is why the steed and saddle selected for me provoked, initially at least, peals of laughter among our small group of riders. My horse looked like a Budweiser Clydesdale, and my saddle looked like a La-Z-Boy recliner with stirrups instead of a footrest. By the third day, however, no one was laughing at me anymore. The other riders were saddle-sore to the bone, and I was still comfy in my La-Z-Boy saddle.

We began our ride in Sancerre, where the vineyards produce one of the world's most elegant white wines. The great tower in town stands in silent tribute to the courage of French Protestants, who withstood a genocidal eight-month siege by Roman Catholic troops during the Wars of Religion in the sixteenth century.

On a typical day, we'd ride for several hours in the morning through ancient forests, verdant hills, and fields filled with Van Gogh sunflowers. Then we'd pull into a tiny village, put our horses in the churchyard, and traipse into the village restaurant for a lunch. Thus fortified, we'd saddle up and ride for another three or four hours until we reached the next destination, where we would have dinner and spend the night. The next morning after breakfast, we'd head off again.

The most memorable evening came on the third day. Our host invited us to join him for dinner. During the soup course, we went around the table and introduced ourselves. One woman, whom I will call Wendy, was traveling alone. She explained that she was a housewife from a small town in suburban New York City and had four children at home, all boys.

"And how is it that your husband allows such an attractive wife to leave his children at home and take a vacation all alone?" our host asked.

After a pause, Wendy replied without affect, "My husband is dead."

Stunned, our host tossed back his Scotch and then effused, "*Pardonnez-moi!* I am so sorry. I did not know."

Silence reigned at the table for a few awkward moments until our host tried to change the topic of conversation.

"So how are Americans feeling about 9/11 these days? Are Americans still worried about terrorism?"

The rest of us waited for Wendy, knowing the answer was only hers to give. Finally, she replied, "Yes, we are still worried about terrorism. You see, my husband died on 9/11."

Horrified, our host recoiled in his chair, mumbled another set of apologies, and then fell silent.

The next morning, as we rode through the forest in a pouring rain, Wendy explained that she had never before needed to tell anyone about her husband. Everyone in her small town knew what had happened. For the first time since 9/11, she was away from her children, the youngest of whom was not yet born when the towers fell.

Then Wendy did something else she had not done in four years. As she recounted our host's embarrassing gaffe, she began to laugh. The rest of us joined in. After four years of mourning, with her husband dead and her children safe, Wendy rode through the rain in a forest in France, laughing.

I'VE BEEN LISTENING to Beethoven's Ninth Symphony all my life, and my love for its triumphant final movement has only deepened over the years. Beethoven wrote the symphony in Vienna during the early 1820s, when repressive autocrats had been restored to power throughout much of Europe. Beethoven suffered from several debilitating medical conditions that likely contributed to his alcoholism, from which he died in 1827. Given all the personal and political burdens he had to bear, he could have ended his final symphony on a muted note.

But he didn't. He chose as a text the poem "Ode to Joy" by Friedrich Schiller, which opens this chapter:

> *Joy, in Nature's wide dominion,*
> *Mightiest cause of all is found;*
> *And 'tis joy that moves the pinion,*
> *When the wheel of time goes round.*

On these terms, the experience of joy indicates that we've tapped in to the "mightiest cause of all"—the most powerful source of optimism and hope. It reveals that we are living with gratitude for what we have been given, no matter how difficult our circumstances. It also reveals that we've developed a deep awareness of all that yet remains possible.

The inevitable counterpoint of pain and promise that we experience throughout our lives reminds me of four lines from a poem by the nineteenth-century British poet William Blake. He wrote:

> *Joy and woe are woven fine,*
> *A clothing for the soul divine;*

> *Under every grief and pine*
> *Runs a joy with silken twine.*

Blake wrote this poem in 1860, one year after the novelist Charles Dickens, who was also British, wrote *A Tale of Two Cities*. As you may recall, Dickens began his novel with these justifiably famous lines: "It was the best of times, it was the worst of times, it was the age of wisdom, it was the age of foolishness, it was the epoch of belief, it was the epoch of incredulity, it was the season of Light, it was the season of Darkness, it was the spring of hope, it was the winter of despair. . . ."

Blake's poem echoes this "worst of times" sense of despair and woe. He described caged birds, starving dogs, beggars at the gate, a rapacious state, and so on. The main focus of the poem, however, isn't the woe. It's the silken twine of joy that's woven through all human experiences, even the most difficult ones.

Blake titled his poem "Auguries of Innocence." An augury is a prophecy or prediction. The word *innocent* was originally not a moral or legal term but a medical one. It meant uninjured or unharmed. The purpose of the poem, on these terms, is to foretell how we can remain unharmed by human wickedness.

Here's Blake's answer:

> *To see a World in a Grain of Sand,*
> *And a Heaven in a Wild Flower,*

*Hold Infinity in the palm of your hand*
*And Eternity in an hour.*

In order to find joy in life, Blake said, you need to be infinitely attentive to the single glorious thing in front of you, whether it's an hour, a flower, or a grain of sand. You need to focus fully on whatever you happen to be holding in your hand. When you do, you'll see how it relates to everything else: a grain of sand to the rest of the world, a flower to the skies that water it, an hour to the rest of time. In each case, a long chain of causes and consequences extends out to infinity and back to eternity. Sometimes what we see makes us grateful for everything that made it possible. At other times, what we see fills us with shame, anger, or sadness. Often, our experience will be a blend of joy and woe.

Joy often finds expression as beauty in situations of great ugliness. Compelling poetry in response to profound loss, sublime music in response to senseless tragedy, beautiful art in response to desperate wickedness, human harmony in the face of natural disasters: These expressions of joy emerge when our awareness has produced a deep sense of gratitude. By not shielding ourselves from the pain of what's present, we open ourselves to the joy of what's possible. By our example, we invite others to the experience of joy as well.

\*

IF YOU ASK people to describe their ultimate goal in life, most name something other than joy. Some talk about the well-being of their immediate family, financial success, or distinction in their chosen field of endeavor—external indicators of success. Others talk about experiencing pleasure or achieving happiness—internal indicators of success. Both indicators have their advantages, and both have their shortcomings.

External indicators of success have the advantage of being relatively easy to measure. You can state your net worth, describe how your parents or children are doing, show pictures of your grandchildren, or say when you were last promoted. But none of these factors alone, nor all of them together, necessarily indicates how your life as a whole is going. Even if everything looks fine on the outside, you may be miserable on the inside. And even if things aren't going well in objective terms, you may nonetheless feel satisfied.

Pleasure and happiness, in contrast, are inner experiences. They're ways of feeling. Both have impeccable credentials as key indicators of human well-being. The ancient Greek philosopher Epicurus taught that the ultimate goal of human life was to avoid pain and pursue pleasure. The U.S. Declaration of Independence declares that the pursuit of happiness is an unalienable right. While both experiences are indeed good to have, pleasure seems too fleeting, and happiness seems too fickle (happiness shares its root meaning with haphazard and happenstance) for either to serve as the ultimate goal of living. In addition, both pleasure and happiness seem rather too narcissistic to set as the ultimate goal of a way of life intended to be all-encompassing. Besides, some people seem to derive pleasure from hurting other people.

Unlike pleasure and happiness, the experience of joy has typically been described in spiritual terms. It features prominently in various religious traditions as a key quality demonstrated by people who are spiritually mature. The experience of joy springs from a deep sense of satisfaction—but not necessarily with the way things in our lives and world happen to be at the moment. Rather, it springs from a deeply engaged openness to what's present, along with a broadly imaginative sense of what's possible. Joyful people feel deeply connected to the people and world around them, whether things are wonderful or terrible—and maybe especially if they're terrible. They see the pain of what's present, but they also know that something better is possible. Best of all, they know that they can help.

In this way, joyful people feel profoundly connected to the unfulfilled promise that the future represents. Most important, they feel deeply engaged in connecting the two. Joyful people serve as a conduit uniting what's present with what's possible. Joy comes when people know that they are essential to the creative advance of time into the future.

In my experience, people experience deep and abiding joy when they are in the place where they should be, doing what they should be doing. They are pursuing what's best. No matter the outcome, they feel joyful when engaged in doing the work that most needs to be done.

Experiences of joy give a foretaste, albeit fleeting and fragmentary, of an ideal that beckons us onward, a picture of how life ultimately could be. These experiences give a glimpse of the kind of individuals we seek to become and the kind of world we seek to create. When we experience true joy, we know that we are living with gratitude.

## PART TWO

The Hallmarks of Gratitude

# CHAPTER 6

# *Gratitude Connects Everything*

২৮

Not wholly this or that,
But wrought
Of alien bloods am I,
A product of the interplay
Of traveled hearts.
Estranged, yet not estranged, I stand
All comprehending;
From my estate
I view earth's frail dilemma;
Scion of fused strength am I,
All understanding,
Nor this nor that
Contains me.

GEORGIA DOUGLAS JOHNSON (1880–1966),
"COSMOPOLITE"

SEVERAL YEARS AGO, Holly and I spent a weekend in Chicago visiting Zoë and her then fiancé and now husband, Connor. One afternoon, we were walking around the campus of the University of Chicago, where Connor was studying for his PhD in econometrics. As we proceeded on our meander through the main quadrangle, we came upon Swift Hall, which houses the Divinity School. Holly commented that she had never been inside Swift Hall, even though she had attended my PhD graduation outside on the quadrangle lawn a decade or so earlier.

We entered Swift Hall, and I began showing her around. When we reached the third floor, I opened the door to a seminar room in one corner of the building and invited Holly to step inside.

I was completely unprepared for my reaction that followed. Tears began flowing down my cheeks, and I felt overcome with emotion. For a few moments, I couldn't speak. Holly broke the silence by saying, "This is where you first studied Whitehead." She didn't have to ask the question. I nodded that she was correct.

In discovering Alfred North Whitehead in that seminar room several decades ago, I found my intellectual and spiritual North Star. An early-twentieth-century Cambridge mathematician who later became a philosopher and theologian at Harvard, Whitehead was equal parts scientist and theologian. He showed me how to think about spirituality and ethics in the modern world.

For a theologian, Whitehead had an unusually profound understanding of the natural world. A mathematician by training, Whitehead collaborated with Bertrand Russell in writing *Principia Mathematica*, widely viewed as one of the most important books of the twentieth century. Whitehead's major philosophical work, published in 1929 under the title *Process and Re-*

*ality,* takes with utmost seriousness the insights of Einstein's theory of relativity. Even more recent scientific developments such as string theory seem almost to have been anticipated by Whitehead's philosophy.

For a scientist, Whitehead had an unusually profound understanding of spirituality and the divine. From a close reading of the book of nature, Whitehead argued that one cannot account for the creative advance of time and history without an understanding of the role of the divine, which Whitehead called God. Beginning not with revelation but with observation, Whitehead built a bridge across the centuries-old divide between matter and spirit, between science and religion, between fact and value, between knowledge and faith, between metaphysics and ethics.

Whitehead's central insight is that *everything becomes whatever it becomes by virtue of how it relates to everything else.* Whether you are a photon, a person, or even God, your identity over time develops through a process of relating to everything else.

Through his work, Whitehead developed a deep confidence in the order of nature, "the faith that at the base of things we shall not find mere arbitrary mystery." Whitehead added, "To experience this faith is to know that our experience, dim and fragmentary as it is, yet resonates with the utmost depths of reality."

These were the words that I had for years longed to hear—hence my reaction in the seminar room. I had wanted reassurance that my confidence in the order of nature was well placed. I had wanted to know that my experience resonates with the depths of reality—with the way things really are.

The founding principle of all existence is this: Everything is constituted by relationships. If you could disassemble the material universe into its constituent elementary particles (there are currently twelve: six quarks and six leptons) and pack them tightly together, you'd have a mere handful of material. (It's hard to believe, but this is literally true.) Everything else is relationships: the experience of these particles as they relate to each other.

Whitehead insisted that what's true of the physical world is also true of the spiritual world. Just as atoms are never lost in physical reactions, so no human experience—however sad or tragic—is ever suffered alone or eternally forgotten. Once something has happened, it remains forever part of the experiences that make up existence as we understand it. As Whitehead put it, everything that happens in the universe—"its sufferings, its sorrows, its triumphs, its immediacies of joy"—is woven into the harmony of a completed whole. Whitehead termed this binding element, which unites everything and ensures that all experiences have an enduring refuge, God.

This is not the God of the patriarchs or any traditional religion. Rather, it's Whitehead's way of describing spiritual experience at its most comprehensive and most profound. It's a feeling—and Whitehead described it as a feeling, not as a person or an idea. I describe it as the ultimate spiritual experience. It's the experience of being deeply connected to everything: all that is present in our lives and our world, as well as all that is past and all that is possible. When I use the term God, which I occasionally do, I do so in this sense: as the experience of ultimate belonging.

In order for the universe to exist as it does, the many elements have to be connected in one particular way at each particular moment, held together by nuclear, electromagnetic, and gravitational forces. By the next moment, things have changed somewhat, so everything has to be connected in a somewhat different way. But the process is the same. The many elements that constitute the universe become one moment of experience, in which everything is ultimately connected to everything else in one particular way. In so doing, the universe thereby *gains* another moment of experience. In Whitehead's words, "The many become one and are increased by one."

This is the fundamental process by which events take place and time moves forward. Everything is ultimately connected to everything else. In a culture that continually touts individuality and self-reliance as defining virtues, it's a counterintuitive claim that we are defined not by how we are independent of the people and world around us, but by how we are connected to them. It's a claim that happens to be true.

As the Harlem Renaissance poet Georgia Douglas Johnson says in the poem that opens this chapter, "I stand / All comprehending." Three lines later, Johnson adds, "Scion of fused strength am I, / All understanding." This turns out to be a crucial juxtaposition.

Johnson begins by acknowledging that she is not wholly this or that, but wrought of alien bloods, a product of the interplay of traveled hearts. All this she grasps, or takes in, or comprehends.

This interrelated state of affairs, she says, is Earth's frail dilemma: Everything is the product of interplay—of one thing and another, of this and that. In that way, she concludes, I get my strength from being fused to everything else—from being a cutting or a shoot (the meaning of scion) off the tree of life that sustains me. All this, she says, I understand. Because I'm fused to everything else, I also understand that no one thing fully contains me.

Everything interplays as part of an undivided whole. Yet each person—and each thing—occupies a unique place and plays a unique role within the vast universe of relationships that make up existence as we know it. In personal terms, I am related to everyone and everything in a unique way.

This means that I'm not a peripheral part of the world I inhabit. Rather, I'm central: There exists an entire universe of relationships, both natural and human, with me playing the central role. My response needs to be more than just adding carbon dioxide and organic waste.

In order to survive, I take energy and resources from the natural world. If I'm fortunate, I have what I need to flourish. My gratitude goal in response should be to ensure that the various ecosystems in the natural and human world also can survive, and maybe even flourish.

At the physical level, I am connected to everyone and everything else through the vast universe of relationships that constitute existence as we know it. At the spiritual level, I am connected to everyone and everything else through gratitude—gratitude for the experiences these connections make possible.

The more I take personally the needs of the natural world, the deeper my sense of meaning. The more I understand how I'm part of the world around me, the clearer my sense of purpose. The more I experience the world I'm part of, the more abiding my sense of joy.

AT THE SPIRITUAL level, the various elements that make up the world of my experience aren't held together by electromagnetism or gravity, but by gratitude. As human beings, we have all come from the natural world around us (our source), and we will all eventually return to it (our destiny). Whether in its solid form as earth, its liquid form as water, its gaseous form as air, or its fiery form as energy, the natural world isn't just where we exist; it's how we exist and of what we exist. We are wholly constituted by the various elements of the natural world. If anything deserves our deepest gratitude, it is this unbelievably vast cosmos—intricate, well ordered, and complete—that we call our home.

The most ancient forms of human spirituality happen to be earth-centered traditions, and rightly so. The epithet "Mother Earth" makes the point precisely: We are formed within and from the natural world, and we are nurtured by it. The practice of gratitude calls us to a spiritual way of living that returns the natural world to its rightful place of reverence.

Tragically, reverence for the natural world has mostly been cast aside. In the centuries since the Industrial Revolution, we've abused the earth with increasingly wanton abandon. We've poisoned the ground, contaminated the water, and polluted the air, not to mention denuding vast swaths of the earth and draining the oceans of precious resources. In some areas, the natural world is beginning to fail as a suitable habitat for humanity and other creatures of the earth and sea.

The practice of gratitude asks me to take this situation personally. This is easier said than done, but it's less a matter of know-how than it is of willpower. We mostly know what needs to be done to restore and safeguard our planetary ecosystem. The challenge lies in galvanizing ourselves to do so.

As the British botanist Michael McCarthy points out in his book *The Moth Snowstorm: Nature and Joy,* the efforts to defend and protect the natural world based on what is sensible and responsible haven't been successful, nor have efforts based on what's in our economic self-interest. It's time for another way, McCarthy says, "something different entirely: we should offer up what it means to our spirits; the love of it. We should offer up its joy."

After all, he goes on to say, human beings have been sitting in towns and cities, staring into computer screens, for only a single generation. We've been working in neon-lit offices for only three or four generations. But before that we were farmers for five hundred generations, and before that we were hunter-gatherers for perhaps fifty thousand or more generations. We lived with the natural world and evolved as part of it. That legacy can't easily be done away with.

But we do need to reconnect to the natural world. We do so, McCarthy insists, through experience of it. He says, "I think deep down the feeling is that we are astonished to be in a world which can contain such a phenomenon—the nightingale singing in the darkness, say—and somehow, the astonishment then reaches out beyond the sense of our place in the world, merely, to the fact that we exist at all."

I have my own catalog of astonishment. I'll never forget the first time I saw a wood duck, an exquisite creature of such impossibly extravagant beauty that I could hardly believe what I was looking at. The experience makes me recall the science writer Timothy Ferris's comment about Saturn, which is another breathtaking sight, especially when its rings are tilted earthward. In his book *Seeing in the Dark*, Ferris says that some people "call Saturn too good to be true, whatever that may mean."

I also remember a Christmas Day walk through a state park on eastern Long Island when my daughter, Zoë, was a toddler. The sun was shining, the air was crystal clear, and the frozen ground was covered by a thin blanket of fresh snow. Zoë was riding on my shoulders, and we were scattering sunflower seeds we had brought along to feed the birds.

As we walked, we came upon several pairs of chickadees, which flitted down from the bare branches for seed. Standing silently still and whispering for Zoë to hold still as well, I held out my hand, seed at the ready. After a few test flights to scout the landing, one chickadee alighted on my hand and snatched up a seed. Then another came, and then another—feather-light landings in a whisper of wings. Zoë was mesmerized, and I was too.

I could go on. A magical moonrise late one night over the sea on a beach where Long Island meets the

Atlantic Ocean. A phantasmagorical fireball during the Perseid meteor shower during the middle of the night in a meadow in upstate New York. These experiences and others like them produce dual feelings of astonishment—that the world contains such marvelous moments and that I am fortunate enough to be part of such a world.

These experiences, McCarthy rightly concludes, are experiences of joy. He says, "My sense of it is of an emotion by which we are overcome, comparable to the religious experience, on the one hand, or the aesthetic experience, on the other, and it signifies that there is something very special to us about its object, perhaps through what that object makes us feel about our place in the world." McCarthy refers to this feeling of joy as "a concentrated happiness." Quoting the eighteenth-century German philosopher Immanuel Kant, McCarthy adds that joy involves "an astonishment which does not cease when the novelty wears off."

Nor, hopefully, does our effort cease to nurture and sustain the world that makes these experiences possible. Our gratitude goal each day should be to take personally, each in our own way, the needs of the natural world.

# CHAPTER 7

# Gratitude Emphasizes Relationships

ॐ

. . . no, your history doesn't smell sweet
Like a toddler's head. But look

at those small round wrists,
that short-legged, comical walk.
Caress your history, touch its hair.
Promise to come back later.

Pay attention when it asks you
simple questions: Where are we going?
Is it scary? What happened? Can
I have more now? Who is that?

JEREDITH MERRIN (B. 1944),
EXCERPT FROM "FAMILY REUNION"

DURING THE SUMMER of 2000, the descendants of my maternal grandparents, Eli and Amelia Swartzentruber, gathered in Delaware for a family reunion. Since there were two hundred of us, more or less (and another hundred or so were unable to attend), we met at Greenwood Mennonite School, which I had attended through the third grade. My then-fiancée, Holly (we married later that year in November), went along to meet my extended family for the first time. She was stunned by the numbers. If the analogous group of her relatives had gathered, she said, there would have been eleven people in the room.

In order to ensure that everyone was fed amply and efficiently, the eight sibling families represented were each assigned duties at one of the mealtimes. My mother's family, along with the family of her next-older brother David, was assigned to clean up after lunch. As I recall, I was in the kitchen washing pots and pans when Uncle David sidled up next to me bearing a stack of dirty dishes. He set the dishes down, and then he turned to me and asked, "When are you going to stop committing adultery?"

"What you mean?" I asked.

"The Bible says that adultery is a sin," he replied. He nodded toward Holly and asked again, "When are you going to stop committing adultery?"

"Uncle David," I responded, "we're not committing adultery."

"What do you mean?" he retorted. "You're living together, aren't you? You must be committing adultery."

"But we're not," I replied. "You have to be married in order to commit adultery, and we're not married. What we're doing is fornicating."

Uncle David responded with a splutter and then suddenly developed a pressing need to clean up a table in the far corner of the dining hall.

I was not the first member of my generation to stray from the straight and narrow. By the time I became an adult, some of my older cousins had already wandered away from the Conservative Mennonite Church, and several had even gotten divorced. With one or two notable exceptions, their parents had reacted with variations on the theme sounded by Uncle David. When one of his own children got divorced, Uncle David initially forbade her from ever entering the family home again.

Fortunately for me, my mother took a different approach. She saw how destructive—not to mention ultimately futile—the censorious approach could be. She and my father, while they were deeply hurt by my decision to leave the church and get divorced, decided to express divine love as best they could, rather than meting out their version of divine justice. I remain profoundly grateful for their generosity of spirit and their love.

When I think of the chaotic constellation of relationships that make up my own life, Jeredith Merrin's poem "Family Reunion" comes to mind. Set amid a contemporary gathering of an extended family replete with step- and half-relationships, Merrin wryly makes the point earlier in the poem that family reunions aren't what they used to be. Especially for someone like myself who has been married three times and divorced twice, her observation that everyone has grown used to the idea of divorce rings true. But then again, perhaps families never were what they used to be—even when the divorce rate was almost nonexistent.

It's easy to surmise that things could have once been different. Merrin speaks wistfully of our separation "from the landscape of a childhood," as if childhood represents an innocent time when our relationships weren't sliced and diced as they are today. With increasingly rare exceptions, childhoods aren't sweet smelling like a baby's head, nor are family histories.

For Merrin, there is no walking away from our stories, which is why she asks, "What if you turned back for a moment / and put your arms around yours?" What if you pay attention when it asks you simple questions—questions like: What happened? Where are you going?

What happened in my case? I became the person I am today. My experience growing up Mennonite emphasizes how completely my experiences of other people and the natural world make me who I am. These relationships aren't superficial or peripheral. They aren't add-ons to a self that I somehow establish independently of them. Rather, my relationships make me who I am. If you change any of those relationships, you change the person I have turned out to be. Without them, I simply wouldn't exist—at least, not as Galen Guengerich.

Merrin's backward-looking simple question "What

happened?" reflects her forward-looking simple question "Where are we going?" The answer is: from what's past to what's possible. None of us is merely the sum total of all the experiences we have already had. We aren't bystanders in our own self-creation. We are made up of more than just our past relationships and experiences. We are also made up of the possibilities we represent. In order to maximize the value of human experience, both for ourselves and for those around us, our gratitude goal should be to increase the quality of our relationships.

What makes some relationships better than others? Alfred North Whitehead once said that the goal of civilization is the evocation of intensities. By this, he means that the positive physical, emotional, and spiritual relationships that constitute us become more valuable as they become more intense—that is, more substantial and more reciprocal. They become more substantial as each party brings more value to the relationship. And they become more reciprocal as each party benefits more from the relationship.

In light of this scale of value, our gratitude goal should be to increase the quality of our relationships. As we become more fully and deeply engaged with the people around us, we add more value to our own lives, as well as to theirs.

*

WOULD I CHANGE any of my relationships if I could? If I could edit my past, I would be tempted to take out the hard things: the failures, the disappointments, the losses, and yes, maybe even the divorces. But those relationships, and perhaps especially those, are the crucible within which my character was forged. If I had never experienced failure, disappointment, loss, or divorce, I would be a fundamentally different person.

In his book *The View From Here*, the Berkeley philosopher R. Jay Wallace examines the tension we experience between outcomes we hope for and outcomes that happen. As we have already noted, this tension plays out within the framework of meaning that arbitrates between our aspirations and the realities of our lives as they happen. Wallace is particularly interested in regret: what we should regret and what we shouldn't. Words spoken in anger or deeds done out of malice, these we should regret, as we should our failure to act because of negligence or laziness.

But regret should have limits. Wallace cautions against regretting bad things that end up making good things possible. He illustrates this point by asking us to consider the existence of someone we love. He writes, "We can . . . readily imagine that somewhere along the line, the actual ancestors of those we love would not even have encountered each other if not for historical events that were momentously disastrous: a catastrophic and pointless war, for instance, that forced a distant progenitor into the refugee camp where she met her future husband, or a natural calamity of some kind that had a similar effect. Under these conditions, our unconditional affirmation of the person we love will commit us to affirming the objectionable historical conditions that were necessary for the individual person's existence."

I know this to be true from personal experience. An intensive-care nurse named Lynn Raynor took care of my niece—the one who died—during one of her surgeries over the years. Lynn eventually married my younger brother Evan, and today they have two children of their own, Noah and Lydia. Without Krista's tumor, Evan and Lynn wouldn't be married, and Noah and Lydia wouldn't exist.

The story of my relationship with Zoë's mother didn't turn out to be the story either of us intended, but it's the story that happened. It includes both a daughter and a divorce. While I'm deeply sorry for the pain I caused Zoë's mother, Wallace would say that I shouldn't regret the failed relationship unless I'm also willing to regret the daughter, which I'm not. Zoë has become a magnificent woman of whom I am inordinately proud. Again, without a relationship that ended in divorce, there would be no Zoë.

Our relationships—all of them—have made us who we are. The spiritual practice of openness invites us to respond with gratitude even when difficult people and difficult relationships come our way.

Make no mistake: No one should be treated badly, nor should we respond to bad things that happen to us as though they are good, which they are not. Rather, we should affirm these experiences as *our* experiences, and we should recognize that good things can come as a result.

ESPECIALLY GIVEN THE self-centric approach that dominates life in the modern world, we tend to view our relationships instrumentally. We focus on how useful or obstructive others are to helping us get what we want. Each person in our lives has a functional role: customer, sibling, competitor, parent, employee, investor, teacher, friend, boss, teammate, or subordinate. (We also tend to view the elements of the natural world in an instrumental way: Air is for breathing, water is for drinking, land is for developing, trees are for harvesting, oil is for drilling, crops are for engineering, and so on.) Except for close friends and colleagues, we aren't often interested in the person behind the role. If we get what we need or want from them, we're satisfied with the relationship. From our perspective, it's a good relationship.

This approach to relationships leaves us spiritually disconnected from the people around us. Imagine going to the grocery store, David Foster Wallace suggests in his book *This Is Water*. It's the end of an exhausting day in the middle of an exasperating week. You are hungry, tired, and desperate to get home. The store is crowded, the light is harsh, the lines are long, and everyone is annoying. In this situation, Wallace says, "my natural default setting is that situations like this are really all about *me,* about my hungriness and my fatigue and my desire to get home." And who in the world are all these people, and why are they in my way? That's what happens, he says, "when I'm operating on the automatic, unconscious belief that I am the center of the world and that my immediate needs and feelings are what should determine the world's priorities."

There is another option: "I can choose to force myself to consider the likelihood that everyone else in the supermarket's checkout line is probably just as bored and frustrated as I am, and that some of these people actually have much harder, more tedious or painful lives than I do." Maybe the man yelling into his cellphone has a son in prison. Maybe the woman blocking the aisle to the ice cream freezer has just been laid off. Maybe the impossibly slow checkout clerk has just been dumped by her boyfriend.

As human beings, Wallace goes on to say, we are able to *choose* what we pay attention to and how we construct meaning. These choices involve "attention, and awareness, and discipline, and effort, and being able truly to care about other people and to sacrifice for them." The key, he concludes, is awareness: awareness of what is real and essential, what's hidden in plain sight all around us.

This shift from inbound attention on the center of the world (ourselves) to outbound attention on the rest of the world marks the transition from the secular to the spiritual. In spiritual terms, I am constituted by awareness—in this case, my awareness of other people being present not just near me, beside me, or in front of me, but as part of me. It also marks a shift from viewing relationships through the lens of transactions of various sorts (financial, physical, emotional, and sexual) to viewing relationships through the lens of love.

In spiritual terms, love isn't a matter of physical intimacy or even emotional attraction. The late British novelist and philosopher Iris Murdoch, in her essay "The Sublime and the Good," says that "love is the extremely difficult realization that something other than oneself is real." Whatever happens between me and another person emerges not only because of who I am and what I need. It emerges because of the very specific nature of my relation to another person who is very real and very much not me. This person has a different history than I do, different hopes and fears, and different ways of dealing with the vicissitudes of life.

Relationships never happen in general. They always develop between two very particular people. If the two people are fortunate, they both realize that the other person is also real.

The French linguist and feminist scholar Luce Irigaray makes a similar point when she talks about the language we use in relation to each other. Much of the time we use transitive verbs and direct objects that operate like a one-way street: "I hit the ball." Used in this way, the movement of words from one person to the next either subjugates or motivates the object we address: "Susan, please write the report." "Carlos, please clean your room." The goal of this form of speech isn't to establish a connection with another person whose experience is as real and valid as our own. It's to get the other person to see what we want them to see, or do what we want them to do.

Love operates in a different domain, one that is spiritual rather than transactional. The goal of love isn't to get something done. It's to develop the awareness that someone else is not just an object to manipulate or control, but a real subject. Recognizing that another person is both different and real, according to Irigaray, means "respecting you as an other, accepting that I must draw myself to a halt before you as something insurmountable, a mystery, a freedom that will never be mine."

This recognition begins a new way of relating, one based not on manipulation of an object, but on communication with another subject. Irigaray titled her book *I Love to You*. Put simply, she's trying to point out the difference between "I hit the ball" and "I listen to you."

In spiritual terms, our gratitude goal should be to relate to other people in ways that honor who they are as individuals, rather than focusing merely on what they can do for us. We should act in loving ways toward everyone. The goal is to feel connected—not transactionally, but deeply—to the people we encounter each day.

I can feel grateful to the checkout clerk for helping me purchase my almond milk and organic blueberries. Beyond that, I can feel grateful that he has helped make my life as I live it possible. Along the way, I can help him feel better about being part of my life, even if briefly, which might help him feel better too—even if he has just failed his chemistry midterm.

THE GOAL OF increasing the quality of our relationships may sound daunting. But we don't have to attend to all of our relationships at once. In fact, we can't. If we practice openness and gratitude toward the people we encounter each day, we must do so one moment at a time and one person at a time.

One of the best parables I know illustrates this point. It's the story of Lexie McCain, the main character in a book titled *Just One Thing* by the romance novelist Holly Jacobs. After their daughter Grace died young of cancer, Lexie and her husband eventually divorced, driven apart by their shared suffering. When time and circumstances eventually merged their paths once again, they gave marriage another try, a fledgling triumph of hope over history brought to an even more painful end when he died in a car accident, a probable suicide brought on by depression.

In the wake of these devastating losses, Lexie retreated to her family's cabin deep in the woods. She lived there alone, tending her garden and weaving tapestries at her loom. Once in a while, she would venture into town to buy a few essentials. But otherwise, Lexie withdrew completely from the world.

Then, one Monday night after four months alone, she walked two miles into town and took a seat on a barstool in a tavern called The Corner Bar. She chose the stool farthest from the door, hoping to be left alone. She ordered one Killian's Red draught from the bartender, a man named Sam. She drank the beer slowly and then walked back home. This night in town became a routine: always the same bar stool, always one Killian's Red and never more than one, and always on Monday nights.

Why Mondays? Lexie explained, "Fridays and Saturdays were for dates and desperate people looking to 'hook up' with others. I wasn't dating, nor was I interested in hooking up. Sundays were for church, and it seemed wrong to go to a bar that day, even though I wasn't attending church anymore . . . God and I weren't on speaking terms. Still, no bars for me on Sundays. Midweek was filled with work around the cottage. So, Mondays were my day."

After six months of serving Lexie on Monday nights without question or comment, Sam's curiosity overcame her obvious reticence. He paused before he set her beer down and said, "Tell me just one thing." Lexie decided that telling him one thing about herself was easier than arguing with him, so she told him her name.

Thus began a new pattern on Monday nights, to which Sam and Lexie adhered faithfully. "Just one thing," Sam would say as he served her each week, and she would respond by telling him yet another thing about herself. She soon began asking him to say just one thing in return.

Eventually, the things they said to one another began to describe not only the superficial facts about their individual lives, but also the deep suffering they had endured, she as a mother and wife, and he as a badly wounded combat veteran.

Near the end of the book, Lexie says, "I realize now that I am always evolving—always becoming more. And I know that we're all more than just one thing. That I'm more than one thing. That Sam's more than one thing. And maybe the one true thing is that together we are so much more than we are apart. Sometimes the journey to forgiving yourself—to finding yourself—starts with one person, one step . . . with just one thing."

Emotionally and spiritually, our relationships make us who we are. The more substantial and reciprocal they are, the more meaningful and joyful our lives will be. For this reason, our gratitude goal should be to increase the quality of our relationships. We accomplish this goal one person at a time, one interaction at a time.

# CHAPTER 8

# Gratitude Requires Reciprocity

ə∾

What a person desires in life
  is a properly boiled egg.
This isn't as easy as it seems.

BARON WORMSER (B. 1948),
EXCERPT FROM "A QUIET LIFE"

IN MARCH OF 1962, the first Monday of the month dawned in Delaware and New Jersey as an unremarkable late-winter day. The weather forecast called for cool and cloudy weather over the next couple of days with a chance of rain.

Twenty-four hours later, all hell had broken loose—an unexpected cataclysm now known as the Great Atlantic Storm of 1962 or the Ash Wednesday Storm. A fierce nor'easter coming up the coast from Georgia ran into a major snowstorm coming out of the Midwest. Once merged into a single massive storm, it headed north along the Delmarva Peninsula, only to be stopped in its tracks by an arctic cold front barreling down from Canada.

For three days, this vast storm stalled over the Jersey Shore, pounding it with force 10 winds and twenty-five-foot waves. The tides during that period were unusually high perigee tides, which occur every half year when the moon is closest to the Earth. Taken together, these forces combined to wreak more havoc upon the Jersey Shore than any other storm in the twentieth century.

As the Ash Wednesday Storm began in earnest, my mother decided that we needed milk. I was four and a half years old at the time, and we were living on a farm in Delaware, a dozen miles inland from Rehoboth Beach. Dad was somewhere battening down the hatches, so Mom bundled my two-year-old sister and me into our little Ford Falcon, along with a teenage cousin who happened to be around. We headed down the road to a neighbor's dairy farm to fill our empty gallon jar with milk.

As we left the dairy farm, my cousin sat in the front passenger seat holding the gallon of milk in her lap. The wind and rain lashed the car, making it hard for my mother to see where we were going. I recall being quite terrified, especially when a forceful gust of wind caused the car to careen off the road into the ditch. The gallon of milk went flying around the car, as did my sister and I. Miraculously, the jar of milk somehow remained intact, and though none of us were wearing seat belts, we all escaped unscathed as well.

Because my mother was pregnant at the time, our options at that point were few. We feared being stuck in the ditch for the duration. Fortunately, to our enormous relief, someone came along in a pickup truck and pulled us out. We hightailed it back home, where we spent the next several days without power, watching the rain flood the farm and the wind tear at the outbuildings.

But at least we had milk. We also had eggs in the refrigerator from the chicken house, as well as chickens in the freezer that we had processed in the fall (my job was to help pluck the feathers). The freezer also contained cuts of beef and pork from our small herd of cattle and pigs. We had corn and lima beans from the garden in the freezer as well, along with canned pears and plums in the pantry from our orchard, and homemade strawberry jam. (Then as now, I would willingly consume canned pears and plums only as a last-ditch effort to fend off starvation, and even then it would be a close call.) The cold cellar held an ample supply of potatoes, carrots, and onions from the garden.

All told, we could have endured weeks without resupply, if not months. We would definitely have run out of milk, but we could have always headed to the neighbors. Dairy cows need to be milked, no matter the weather.

From the perspective of someone who now lives in a high-rise apartment building in the middle of the city, as I have for the past twenty-seven years, it's easy to view life on the farm as an exercise in self-sufficiency. You can grow your own food! Yet, as Baron Wormser says in his brilliantly insightful poem "A Quiet Life," about what it takes to produce a properly boiled egg, "This isn't as easy as it seems."

Wormser goes on to say you need a stove and a pot, which require mines and furnaces and factories. You need gas to fuel the stove, which requires drills and pipelines and pumping stations, not to mention massive amounts of capital. You need water and salt, and a chicken and some grain. In order for all of these elements to come together in the right way at the right time, you also need political peace. A properly boiled egg? Not so easy.

Strictly speaking, farmers don't grow crops. Warmth and light from the sun, water in the form of rain (or irrigation), and nutrients from the soil (and maybe from fertilizer) enable crops to grow. Farmers till the ground, plant the seeds, and harvest the crops. To do this work, farmers use tractors, harrows, planters, combines, and other machines and equipment, none of which is manufactured by the farmers themselves. Farmers typically apply herbicides and pesticides, which are also manufactured elsewhere, to keep competing plants and inconvenient insects from compromising the crops. The view of life on the farm as self-sufficient, in other words, says far more about the self-sufficient longings of humans who hold this view than it does about life on the farm.

This longing runs deep. From the moment we begin

to breathe on our own as infant human beings, we embark on a quest to do everything else on our own. If fortune has smiled upon us, and we have been born without physical or emotional deficits into a supportive environment, we mostly succeed. We learn to feed ourselves, walk unassisted, go to the bathroom on our own, and give voice to our own thoughts. After a few years, we attend school on our own. In time, we have a job of our own, and then a home of our own. Eventually, we may even have children of our own.

The quest to become physically and emotionally self-sufficient yields remarkable results. At our best, at the height of our powers in the prime of our lives, human beings are remarkable creatures. We have evolved as a species—and then mature as individual human beings—to embody amazing intelligence and exhibit astounding physical capabilities. And we can do it all on our own, or so we say.

Here in America, we have codified this longing into the myth of the "self-made man." Henry Clay, a senator from Kentucky who was running for president, coined the term in 1932 during a three-day speech from the Senate floor. At one point in Clay's address, which he titled "In Defense of the American System," Clay said, "In Kentucky, almost every manufactory known to me is in the hands of enterprising self-made men, who have acquired whatever wealth they possess by patient and diligent labor."

Though Clay's political fortunes took a downturn soon thereafter (Andrew Jackson easily won reelection), his turn of phrase took off. Six years after Clay's speech, Charles Seymour recounted the stories of sixty such men in his book *Self-Made Men*. Harriet Beecher Stowe, author of *Uncle Tom's Cabin*, followed suit in her 1872 book titled *The Lives and Deeds of Our Self-Made Men*. Stowe's book included a profile of her brother Henry Ward Beecher, who extolled self-made virtues from his pulpit at Brooklyn's Plymouth Church.

Beecher, a leading abolitionist during the pre–Civil War era, came to the defense of Andrew Carnegie and other "self-made" industrialists. At a time when the richest 1 percent owned 26 percent of the wealth, and the richest 10 percent owned 72 percent, the workers who actually did the work—mined the ore, refined the steel, and built the railroads, among other enterprises—continually complained of low wages. They said they couldn't even afford butter for their bread on wages of a dollar a day. "Man cannot live by bread alone," Beecher responded in one of his sermons, "but the man who cannot live on bread and water is not fit to live."

Bolstered by the ongoing presence in America of outsize personalities and prodigious wealth, as well as celebratory profiles and laudatory exhortations, the myth of the self-made man has endured, and grown. More recently, the idea has crossed the gender divide. Oprah Winfrey, Nasty Gal founder Sophia Amoruso, and Sheryl Sandberg of Google and Facebook, among others, have established the nascent and growing category of self-made women. Set against the backdrop of our nation's culture of acquisition and consumption, this myth suggests that any one of us, with enough "patient and diligent labor," can make it on our own.

Except that we can't. The image of a human being as self-sufficient is a mirage—the product of wishful thinking. In fact, we rely on the people and the world around us for everything. There is no form of life on earth less self-sufficient than a human being. We can't do anything on our own.

We rely on biological parents for our very existence. We rely on the adults who nurture us—sometimes our biological parents, sometimes not—to shelter us and care for us during our most vulnerable years. We rely on teachers to educate us, nurses and doctors to treat us when we're sick, legislators to enact laws governing our common life, and so on.

We also rely on people in more narrowly focused ways. In order to move safely from place to place, we rely on auto mechanics, oil refinery workers, gas station attendants, road construction workers, and engineers who design stoplights and other traffic control systems. We may also rely on bus drivers and train conductors, as well as pilots and flight attendants.

Most of us, with enough time and enough training, could probably do any one of these individual tasks, or at least many of them. But that's not the point. Rather, the point is that no one of us could do all of them.

Economist Leonard Read illustrates this principle using a different example in his well-known 1958 article titled "I, Pencil." Read claims that not a single person on the face of this earth knows how to make a pencil. It's true, he says, that it only takes some wood, a little paint, a printed label, a line of graphite lead, a bit of metal, and an eraser. But, he goes on to explain, each of these elements requires entire industries to produce—mining, refining, manufacturing, and so on.

This principle also applies to every other aspect of life as we know it. No one of us could do everything necessary to make a car, perform a symphony concert, run a restaurant, or build a smartphone. We rely completely on the people around us, both those close at hand and those far away, for everything that makes our lives possible.

The same principle extends to the natural world. For the air we breathe, we rely on trees and other plants to take in carbon dioxide and give off oxygen, reversing our own cycle. We rely on the sun to warm the atmosphere, generating wind and rain. We rely on plants and animals to provide our daily sustenance.

On the survival end of the spectrum, our needs are unequivocal. We can only survive for a few minutes without air and about ten days without water. Without food, human beings can typically survive for only thirty to forty days, though in a few cases, people have been known to survive for as long as seventy days. Even so, human life requires regular sustenance for survival.

The principle that everything ultimately relies on everything else functions very much like a law of nature. There's no escaping it, anytime or anywhere. Its central insight is that we are contingent creatures. The image of a self-reliant human being, while it may be the icon of Western culture, is a myth. No such person exists—or can exist.

Of course, sometimes our environment doesn't nurture our well-being, but rather destroys it. In these situations we need to find our way elsewhere, to people who are good for us and places that support us. We may require help to make these changes, but they need to be made nonetheless.

Even as we rely on everyone and everything else to make our lives possible and even perhaps enjoyable, the people around us, along with the natural world, rely on us to bear our share of responsibility for the common life we share. In return for all we have been given, we owe something back. Life isn't a one-way system, with everything inbound to us and nothing outbound.

Those of us who aspire to live with gratitude want to live in a way that enables us to feel good about our relationships to the world around us—a way of living that's healthy for us, healthy for plants and animals, and healthy for the earth. Since our need for food and water is nonnegotiable, our challenge is to fulfill both our need for sustenance and our goal of living with gratitude. Besides, eating and drinking establish our closest connection to the earth and its plants and creatures. They become part of us.

We can meet our gratitude goal through awareness of what it requires of the natural world to provide our sustenance. It's my conviction, and my experience, that reciprocity follows awareness. The more aware we become of the interplay between our lives and the world around us, the more gratitude we will feel for all that we continually rely on. Gratitude, in turn, requires reciprocity. We will endeavor to do our part to ensure that the life around us flourishes, even as we are able to flourish. When this happens, we will feel a deep and abiding sense of joy.

EACH OF US as human beings needs to take personally the sources of our food—to know firsthand what the earth and its creatures give for our survival and our physical health. We begin by acknowledging the often-brutal calculus of life: Living things must consume other living things in order to survive. That's the way life happens on this particular planet, in this particular cosmos.

Our culture has given us significant latitude in choosing our individual ways of life, especially when it comes to what we eat and drink. Enormous industries have developed—farming, processing, marketing, and advertising, among others—in order to convince us to eat in a particular way. These industries keep us far removed, often intentionally, from our food at its source. If we knew exactly where food comes from and how it gets to us, we may well end up eating differently than we do.

I have an advantage in this respect. Having grown up on a farm, I know where food comes from and how it gets from farm to table. My dad worked in a slaughterhouse for a short period of time when I was a boy, so I've seen firsthand what happens there too.

In addition, I used to go fishing in my younger days—for flounder when we were living in Delaware and for catfish and bass when we were living in Arkansas. My fondest memories of time spent with my dad and his father came while flounder fishing on the Chesapeake Bay. We'd rent a small boat on the eastern shore of the Chesapeake and head out for the day. I still remember the thrill of hooking flounder and reeling them in. No matter the size, the flounder always felt like "a tremendous fish," as Elizabeth Bishop says in one of her poems.

One reason the flounder felt tremendous has to do with simple fluid dynamics. For its weight, a flounder presents a large amount of surface area. When its flat and rounded body—a flounder looks something like a puffy pancake—is turned sideways to resist being pulled through the water, it feels like a much larger fish. The other reason it felt tremendous, at least to me, was that the flounder was instinctively fighting against the pull of the line—fighting for its life. In my case, the flounder would typically lose.

For the most part, the various food-related industries operating today have little interest in consumers knowing exactly where food comes from and how it ends up in the grocery store or on the table. With rare exceptions their goal is to make a profit by selling us more food, often food that's been highly processed.

In response for all we have been given, we can lighten the load in return. For example, food and beverages that have been processed and packaged exact a much heavier toll on the earth, its creatures, and its people than food and beverages that come to us in more or less their original form.

With water, the toll is already high and continues to climb higher. Ocean acidification and pollution have decimated the well-being of Earth's largest habitat. If current trends continue, there will be more plastic by weight than fish in the world's oceans by 2050. Freshwater pollution and overuse have left many people without access to clean water, a trend exacerbated by those who profit from exploiting this universal human need.

Household use accounts for only about 10 percent

of freshwater consumption worldwide. Industry accounts for about one-quarter or so of freshwater use, a fact we should keep in mind when buying manufactured goods. Since agriculture accounts for about two-thirds of freshwater use, the best way to conserve water may be to change the way we eat. All other things being equal, food made from animals requires vastly more water to produce than food made from plants.

While taking the time to trace the supply chain or follow the money can be useful exercises, they won't stimulate our sense of gratitude, at least not alone. Rather, *gratitude emerges from continual awareness of our many and varied relationships to the natural world—relationships that sustain us and ultimately enable us to live with joy.* If we live attentively, we can have confidence that we will also live responsibly and joyfully.

MY OWN TEMPLATE for mapping my relationships with the natural world comes from a book I've read hundreds of times—and that's no exaggeration. I suppose it's theoretically possible for a toddler to go to sleep without having read *Goodnight Moon* at least a time or two. But it's unlikely, and it seldom happened when Zoë was growing up. Margaret Wise Brown's 1947 classic says everything that needs to be said about going to bed.

The book begins with a survey of the known universe, the great green room, identifying each item in the room by name. Once this universe has been mapped, then the business of going to sleep begins in earnest. The process involves a single ritual: saying goodnight to each thing in turn. The book concludes, "Goodnight stars, goodnight air, goodnight noises everywhere."

That's the end of the book. Everything in the great green room has been named and received its benediction. The geography of the toddler's universe has been mapped, and all the relationships within it made clear. There's nothing more to do but fulfill the purpose of this ritual, which is to go to sleep.

As children grow older, the dimensions of the universe expand dramatically in both space and time. The walls of the great green room move outward to include the earth, and then the solar system, and eventually the universe itself. Bedtime marks only one moment in a life that eventually becomes woven into the story of everything that exists. Growing up is a process of learning that the universe is unimaginably vast and infinitely complex. It's also a process of learning how much we rely on the world around us, and how much the human-ravaged natural world now needs our help in return.

Just because we've grown up doesn't mean we shouldn't continue pronouncing a benediction—the word originally meant to wish well or to bless—on the plants, creatures, and other elements that make up the world of our experience.

Robin Wall Kimmerer, in her book *Braiding Sweetgrass: Indigenous Wisdom, Scientific Knowledge, and the Teachings of Plants,* refers to the Native American tradition of blessing the sources of their sustenance. It's a tradition that's well worth emulating. I realize the sun won't respond in kind if you walk out the door in the morning and, seeing it beaming once again in the sky, breathe a silent "Thank you, sun" or "Bless you, sun." Then again, perhaps the warmth and light it offers to you are blessing enough. Thank you, wind. Thank you, clouds. Thank you, rain. Thank you, trees. And so on.

Mealtime offers an especially good opportunity to renew our awareness of how much we rely on sources of life beyond ourselves. It's a sobering realization that everything we eat (with a few obvious exceptions, such as water and salt) was once alive. The least we can do is pause to acknowledge our gratitude for the claim our need for sustenance makes on other life-forms. Thank you, blueberry bush. Thank you, pear tree. Thank you, milk cow. Thank you, cornstalk.

The late Andre Dubus was an award-winning writer who lost his leg in an automobile accident. In his book *Meditations from a Movable Chair,* he tells about making sandwiches on Tuesdays for his second- and seventh-grade daughters and taking the sandwiches to school. He writes:

On Tuesdays when I make lunch for my girls, I focus on this: the sandwiches are sacraments. . . . And each motion is a sacrament, this holding of plastic bags, knife, of bread, of cutting board, this pushing of the chair, this spreading of mustard on bread, this trimming of liverwurst, of ham. All sacraments, as putting the lunches into a zippered book bag is, and going down my six ramps to my car is.

I drive on the highway, to the girls' town, to their school, and this is not simply a transition; it is my love moving by car from a place where my girls are not to a place where they are; even if I do not feel or acknowledge it, this is a sacrament. If I remember it, then I feel it too. Feeling it does not always mean that I am a happy man driving in traffic; it simply means that I know what I am doing in the presence of God.

If I were much wiser, and much more patient, and had much greater concentration, I could sit in silence in my chair, look out my windows at a green tree and the blue sky, and know that breathing is a gift; that a breath is sufficient for the moment; and that breathing air is breathing God.

We have been given the extraordinary gift of being alive in a world that labors tirelessly and without complaining to provide us with everything we need. We should bless the sources of our sustenance every chance we get. We should also do what we can to ensure that they flourish as well.

# CHAPTER 9

# *Gratitude Takes Responsibility*

"I have no time for those things now," we say;
"But in the future just a little way,
No longer by this ceaseless toil oppressed,
I shall have leisure then for thought and rest.
When I the debts upon my land have paid,
Or on foundations firm my business laid,
I shall take time for discourse long and sweet
With those beloved who round my hearthstone meet;
I shall take time on mornings still and cool
To seek the freshness dim of wood and pool,
Where, calmed and hallowed by great Nature's peace,
My life from its hot cares shall find release;
I shall take time to think on destiny,
Of what I was and am and yet shall be,
Till in the hush my soul may nearer prove
To that great Soul in whom we live and move.
All this I shall do sometime but not now—
The press of business cares will not allow."
And thus our life glides on year after year;
The promised leisure never comes more near.

EFFIE WALLER SMITH (1879–1960),
EXCERPT FROM "PREPARATION"

MY FINAL CONVERSATION with the renowned physician and author Henry S. Lodge took place two days before he died at age fifty-eight of prostate cancer. Harry was a winsome and accomplished man, a lover of life and people, a true gentleman, possessed of remarkable talents and outsize enthusiasms. An internist by training, Harry's interest in the aging process led him to become board-certified in gerontology. To Harry's family and his many devoted patients, his death at age fifty-eight felt like a tragedy.

Harry felt otherwise. Harry told me that he didn't feel cheated—despite the fact that his life would be foreshortened by more than two decades. "I've been fortunate beyond my wildest dreams," he said. "A career I never could have imagined, two amazing daughters, and the love of my life—my soulmate, Laura, and her two amazing sons."

He went on to say, "There have been hard things too. But most people have just as many hard things as I have had and not nearly as many good things." He added, "Of course I want more of everything. I'd love to live to eighty-five or ninety. But I don't feel cheated. I've had a wonderful life."

TIME IS THE one truly nonrenewable resource in human experience. Given the cyclical nature of our clocks and calendars, it's easy for us to miss this foundational reality. We are accustomed to ordinary days, which follow the pattern previous days have established. The Earth turns on its axis about once every twenty-four hours, and the daily rising and setting of the Sun on our horizon establishes an elemental rhythm of waking, eating, working, and sleeping. The Earth orbits the Sun once every 365 and one-quarter days, the tilt of its axis occasioning our journey through the four seasons. This annual sweep around the Sun paces the human march toward more distant goals. We catalogue in years the milestones in our lives.

There is yet a third way the Earth moves through time and space. For fifteen billion years, the universe as we understand it has been expanding. As far as we know, the universe will continue to expand for perhaps one hundred trillion years into the future, slowly cooling as it does. There is no cycle to this movement, no daily rotation or seasonal repetition. In the cosmic sense, the Earth's journey is a singular one: It will not pass this way again.

The same is true of our lives as human beings. It turns out that the daily and yearly cycles of time are illusory: None is the same as those that have gone before. Each marks the increments by which we measure the inexorable march of time. Our journey, too, is a singular one. We will not pass this way again.

No one knows why this is true. In his book *The Fab-*

*ric of the Cosmos,* physicist Brian Greene calls the arrow of time one of the deepest unresolved mysteries in modern physics. We take for granted that there is a direction to the way things unfold in time. For example, Greene says, "cream stirred into coffee forms a uniformly tan liquid, but we never see a cup of light coffee unstir and separate into white cream and black coffee. Eggs fall, cracking and splattering, but we never see splattered eggs and eggshells gather together and coalesce into uncracked eggs."

All the known and accepted laws of physics treat both directions in time alike. Anything that can happen in one direction can happen in the other—except that it doesn't. Time moves only forward.

Those of us who aspire to live with gratitude respond to the arrow of time by insisting that we treat each day and moment as a uniquely valuable opportunity. Each comes as a gift—one that will be given only once and never again.

Our tendency, however, as the early-twentieth-century African American poet Effie Waller Smith observes in her poem that begins this chapter, is to put things off. We have no time to think about where our lives are taking us—what we were, what we are, and what we yet shall be. We have no time to wander in the woods or sit alongside a lake, where our spirits can be soothed and our souls hallowed by the peace of nature. We have no time to talk at length with friends or invite them over for dinner. We simply have no time for these things now.

But soon, perhaps very soon, when we have our careers up and running and our businesses established, when our credit card debts are paid and our mortgages are smaller, when the press of work subsides, then we'll have time.

In this way, Smith warns, our work-focused life glides on, year after year. The promised time never comes. Eventually, we find our youth and strength and time have gone, and we must give back the life we spent continually preparing to live.

One key element in the poem is the repeated phrase, "I shall take time . . . I shall take time . . . I shall take time." It suggests clearing our calendars for things that really matter by taking time away from the labors that usually consume us.

But it also suggests taking time—taking hold of it as our own. Carpe diem, as the Romans used to say: Seize the day. Seize this day, seize this hour, seize this moment. I shall take time—this time. It's the only time available to seize, and it's our responsibility to seize it.

As human beings, there is nothing we have been given that is more precious, nor more irreplaceable, than whatever time we're allotted. Our gratitude goal in response should be to make the best of each moment. As fully as we can, for as long as we can, we should live as much as we can. By taking responsibility for how we spend our time, we will end up taking responsibility for everything else in our lives.

As we will see in the next section of the book, spiritual practice plays a crucial role in preparing us to live our lives to the fullest. Joyful living requires both physical and spiritual preparation. The sense of joy that emerges from the experience of gratitude doesn't come from nowhere. It emerges as we realize that life is fleeting, and therefore we must prepare ourselves to seize each precious moment that we have been given. For the most part, gratitude doesn't concern itself with what used to be or might have been, or with what could be or might be. Gratitude keeps us focused on what's possible.

HOLLY AND I once attended the bar mitzvah of a young man I'll call Jonathan, whose parents are friends of ours. For the benefit of those in attendance who were not Jewish, the officiating rabbi explained that under Jewish law, children are not required to observe the commandments, although they are encouraged to study and learn the obligations they will someday have as adults. But at the age of twelve for girls and thirteen for boys, the responsibility to follow the commandments falls on children as well. The bar or bat mitzvah ceremony formally marks the assumption of that obligation, along with the corresponding right to take part in leading religious services. But, the rabbi said, the bar mitzvah ceremony is not required to confer these rights and responsibilities. They come automatically when you become a grown-up.

Near the end of the ninety-minute service, the rabbi stood before Jonathan and addressed him directly concerning what it means to be a grown-up. He talked about how Jonathan stands in a long line of faithful men and women—not just the ones described in the Hebrew Bible, but also his grandparents, who risked their lives to rescue fellow Jews from the clutches of the Nazis, and his parents, who had passed on the tradition with dedication and love. "Now, Jonathan, it's your turn," said the rabbi. "Your responsibility in life is to be a good ancestor to those who will follow after you."

The underlying meaning of the word *responsibility* includes the word *respond*—to make a promise in return for something you have been given. In Jonathan's case, he had been raised within a tradition of faith and faithfulness to which he was now obligated to respond. He made a promise in return about his own life of faith and faithfulness.

Of course, Jonathan could have acted otherwise. He could have taken his spiritual inheritance for granted and acted like it made no claim on him. Or he could have denigrated it as worthless. He did neither, but rather promised to fulfill his responsibility to be faithful.

Each morning when we receive the gift of a new day, we take up anew the responsibility to be faithful— faithful to the possibility each moment brings.

SEVERAL YEARS BEFORE I met Harry Lodge, I came across a book titled *Younger Next Year*, which Harry had co-authored with Chris Crowley. A former litigator, Crowley was in his late fifties and reasonably active. He'd done a lot of skiing during his years in Colorado. But the signs of eventual aging were beginning to affect his waistline, his blood pressure, and his cholesterol count. When he moved from Colorado back to New York, he needed to find a primary care physician.

Crowley ended up making an appointment to see Harry. After the usual exam of poking and prodding, along with drawing blood and addressing lots of vaguely scary questions, the two sat down to chat. Always the interrogating attorney, Chris posed a question: "So, what is it about the practice of medicine that you like most?"

Harry responded, "There is a fundamental revolution at hand in the way people age." In the old days, he said, the assumption was that most people would experience a slow, steady decline from about age fifty or so until they died. This was known as the aging process. Today, he said, we know that this decline usually isn't necessary, and it can often be reversed. Then he said to

Chris, "You could be younger next year in all the ways that matter. Younger next year and for quite a few years to come."

This chance comment led to an ongoing collaboration between the two of them and eventually a book, which to date has sold more than two million copies and has been translated into more than twenty languages. Its premise is that the long slide from being fit and healthy in midlife to physically debilitated and socially isolated at the end of life isn't necessary in most cases. What we typically think of as the necessary effects of aging are mostly the unnecessary effects of neglect.

Harry and Chris summarize the plan for being younger next year in seven succinct rules. The first three rules concern exercise—an hour of vigorous exercise six days a week for the rest of your life (four days of aerobic exercise and two days of strength training). The fourth rule has to do with money: "Spend less than you make." Rule five is about food: "Quit eating crap!" The authors don't define crap, apparently assuming that most of us already know what it is.

Rule six consists of a single word: "Care." You need to care deeply about something beyond your own needs and desires. Rule seven concerns relationships: "Connect and Commit." The quality of the last third of your life will ultimately be determined by the quality of your relationships. Take charge of making them deep and substantial.

If you follow these rules, Harry and Chris insist, you'll be younger next year in all the ways that matter. The change won't happen overnight; you won't be younger next week or next month. But over time you can turn back the clock.

After reading the book, which I found both persuasive and entertaining, I ended up referring to it in a sermon on the decline of religious participation in the United States. Is the religious decline, I wondered, like the decline in physical vitality, expected but unnecessary? After preaching the sermon, the book went on my bookshelf.

I reached for it again when I turned fifty-nine. As I began my final year in my fifties, I looked at myself in the mirror and didn't like what I saw. I had all the challenges Chris Crowley had faced: thirty pounds overweight, blood pressure too high, cholesterol too high, and so on. In addition, I was in the middle of what has thus far turned out to be the most difficult stretch of my professional life, and I was letting the pressure get me down—physically, emotionally, and spiritually. I desperately needed to make a change.

From my perspective, the most important insight of *Younger Next Year* has to do with time and setting priorities. When we're younger, Harry and Chris say, we can get away with treating regular exercise, healthy eating, altruistic involvements, and profound relationships as things we try to do on the margins. Our primary attention tends to be focused on our careers and perhaps our families. As we age, these priorities need to be reversed.

Harry and Chris use exercise as the template for describing the change in priorities. They say, "One of the terrific things about the go-to-work habit is that it's a great prioritizer. Work trumps everything except serious illness or serious family problems. Daily exercise should be treated the same way. If you're going to have success with this excellent new life, you're going to have to give regular exercise that priority."

But, they caution, you can't end up trying to decide each day to make exercise a priority. It has to be a habit, like going to work—something you do without deciding whether or not you're going to do it. They say, "The only real trick is to have a schedule and a habit. No one has the character to make the fresh decision every day to go to the gym. Go on 'automatic' or you'll quit."

Fortunately for me, I was able to take their advice to heart. I started CrossFit, a vigorous and ever-varying combination of cardio, weightlifting, and gymnastics that has remained a steady habit ever since. Whether I'm at home or traveling, I try to arrange my other commitments so I can spend an hour in a CrossFit class or engaged in strength training three or four times a week. As a result, I have lost the thirty pounds I needed to lose, and my blood pressure is now normal. My cholesterol has fallen to a surprisingly low level for a person of my age and heritage, in part because my eating patterns have also been transformed. If you are going to expend energy to tune up your body, there's no reason to fuel it with crap.

These habits have gradually transformed other areas of my life as well. The goal of being physically fit and physiologically healthy, after all, has nothing to do with how fast you can run or how much weight you can lift. *The goal is to be ready to live your life to the fullest. It's to be fully capable of responding to the unique and precious gift of each day and each moment.*

SOME YEARS AGO on a cold night in January, Holly and I had dinner with a couple who were then members of my congregation. One of their daughters (her daughter, his stepdaughter) lived in another part of the country. She was a talented and successful thirty-nine-year-old artist, married with two children under the age of six. She had learned the previous August that she had a virulent form of cancer. A month later, she found out that the cancer had already metastasized.

Over dinner with her parents, we learned that she had between six and nine months to live, a prognosis that turned out to be accurate. At one point during the evening, her neurosurgeon stepfather said, "I find it almost impossible to believe that by this time next year she'll be gone." He paused, as if going over her medical diagnosis and prognosis in his head, then said, "But there's nothing I can do about it."

He went on, "The one comfort I've found comes from the words you say at the end of each service at All Souls: 'This is the day we are given. Let us rejoice and be glad in it.'" He added, "I've said that to a lot of people in the past few weeks. 'This is the day we are given.' We aren't guaranteed any more than this one day."

I have performed enough memorial services and funerals for people who are younger than me to have taken this truism to heart. Some of them died slowly and others suddenly, but all of them found the lives they had expected to live interrupted by death. Sometime, maybe sooner, maybe later, death will come to me as well, and to all of us.

In the meantime, our gratitude goal should be to make the best of each moment. Live each day to the fullest. This is the day we are given. As Henry James once put it, "Live all you can; it's a mistake not to."

# CHAPTER 10

# *Gratitude Creates Beauty*

ڊ

Try to praise the mutilated world.
Remember June's long days,
and wild strawberries, drops of wine, the dew.
The nettles that methodically overgrow
the abandoned homesteads of exiles.
You must praise the mutilated world.

ADAM ZAGAJEWSKI (B. 1945), EXCERPT FROM
"TRY TO PRAISE THE MUTILATED WORLD"

I CAME LATE to the appreciation of beauty as an essential human experience. The aesthetic hierarchy of my Conservative Mennonite upbringing didn't reserve a place for beauty, or at least it wasn't high on the list of priorities. Clean came first, which is why the list of Saturday chores invariably included cleaning your room, polishing your shoes, and washing the car. Useful came next, followed by durable.

Beauty only played a role when it came to describing God's creation (it was fine to say a flower or a sunset was beautiful) or the dwelling place of God in heaven ("where the gates are of pearl, and the streets are of gold, and the buildings exceedingly fair," as my maternal grandmother's favorite hymn puts it). When it came to human beings and human creations, either beauty indicated vanity (human labor produces "vanity of vanities," according to the Hebrew Bible), or it posed a source of temptation (the Christian New Testament warns against "the lust of the flesh, the lust of the eyes, and the pride of life").

Not everyone strictly followed the script. My paternal grandmother, a diminutive and sometimes dour woman named Lulu, had a way with paste wax. Because her sense of value had been forged by the Great Depression, she insisted on rescuing broken toys and disused household items of every kind. Whatever else they needed in the way of repair, these rescued rejects invariably needed a coat of wax—to make them more beautiful, she always said. Grandma had an eye for beauty. She worked hard to leave her corner of the world a little more usable and a little more beautiful.

My father apparently inherited his mother's aesthetic proclivities. He kept a Wollensak reel-to-reel tape recorder and player in the closet, which he would occasionally bring out to play classical music, usually one of Beethoven's symphonies. In a Conservative Mennonite tradition that allowed a cappella singing only (no instruments), this orchestral extravagance provided a rare treat. I don't know if church leaders explicitly forbade this guilty pleasure. My guess is that they treated it like chicken pox: not a problem as long as it didn't spread.

When we moved to southern Arkansas, I began attending a public elementary school. Several weeks later, I brought home a sheaf of papers, one of which was a sign-up sheet for string instrument lessons. To my surprise, my parents asked me if I wanted to learn to play the violin. To their surprise, I said yes.

For the next dozen years or so, music dominated my life—initially orchestral music, then choral music as well. My violin skills progressed enough that I was eventually able to join a string quartet, then a symphony orchestra, and then a light opera company. I ended up playing some of the basic orchestral repertoire, accumulating favorites along the way: Vivaldi's Four Seasons, Bach's Brandenburg Concertos, Schubert's Symphony No. 7 (especially the second movement), and Beethoven's Symphony No. 9, which I had been listening to all my life.

Eventually, especially during my time studying for my PhD at the University of Chicago, I also developed a fondness for blues music. To me, classical music has always captured the sublime beauty of life at its well-orchestrated best. The blues, however, capture the achingly poignant beauty of life when things fall apart.

Some years ago in late December, Holly and I went down to a club in Greenwich Village called Terra Blues to hear the Holmes Brothers, one of my favorite blues bands. Their first tune of the evening surprised everyone. On the night before New Year's Eve in one of the most secular cities in the country, the Holmes Brothers belted out a poignantly powerful rendition of "Take My Hand, Precious Lord," sung a cappella in three-part harmony. The packed house was stunned into almost-reverent silence. The song would have been suitable for Sunday worship at Greenwood Mennonite Church.

But "Take My Hand, Precious Lord" is also a quintessential blues song. It was written by Rev. Thomas Dorsey in response to the death of his wife, Nettie Harper, in childbirth, along with their infant son. "I am tired, I am weak, I am worn," Dorsey wrote. "Through the storm, through the night, lead me on to the light." The beauty of blues music lies in its wholehearted embrace of life's deepest pain, all the while remaining open to the promise of eventual healing, wholeness, and beauty.

I HAVE COME to love the time of day between sunset and darkness—the poignant and evocative time when, as the old hymn says, "Day is dying in the West, heaven is touching Earth with rest." The direct and often harsh light of the midday sun gives way to a soft and luminous glow. Somehow everything seems beautiful. It's too dark to see litter on the streets, peeling paint, or broken windows. Only the highlights of living remain: the outlines of the day coming to a close, filled in by shadows of the gathering dark. The nineteenth-century

Indigenous Canadian poet Emily Pauline Johnson refers to this as the time of "the shadows and the dream-
ing."

Occasionally, late in the afternoon, I leave my desk
for a few minutes and enter the sanctuary to wait with
the light as it passes. The high-vaulted Georgian sanctuary, with its light-colored walls and large arched windows, is lovely at any time of day, but it's especially
beautiful at sundown, the time for the ancient service
of Vespers, also known as evening prayers. In the traditional Christian liturgy, Vespers ("evening") is one of a
series of services throughout the day that begins with
Lauds ("praise") in the morning and ends with Com-
pline ("complete") before bedtime. Over the centuries,
Vespers proved to be the most meaningful service of the
day, hence the most popular with both congregants and
composers.

The services were mostly sung in a style known as
plainchant. In the sixth century, Pope Gregory collected and organized plainchants into the form we
know today as Gregorian chant. It formed the basis for
the magnificent Baroque-era compositions of Monteverdi and Palestrina. We typically hear this music today
on digital streaming services and in concert halls. But it
was composed for sanctuaries, where faithful women
and men gathered to mark the passing of the day.

Each service interweaves hymns with chanted psalms
and gospel readings. The prayers come toward the

end—prayers of gratitude, of petition, of blessing. One text by Monteverdi captures the spirit of the service when the faithful sing together, "Hear, O heaven, hear my words full of longing and pervaded by joy."

People continue to gather for Vespers because the service captures an important element of human experience. The service symbolizes the confluence of light and darkness, of knowledge and ignorance, of time and eternity. The music nurtures a sense of awe in the face of everything we know and a sense of mystery in the face of everything we do not. Experiences like these open us to the presence of beauty in other forms, and its counterpoint, the presence of ugliness, which appears in many forms as well.


TWO WEEKS AFTER the terrorist attacks of September 11, 2001, *The New Yorker* published a poem by the contemporary Polish poet Adam Zagajewski. Titled "Try to Praise the Mutilated World," the poem captures both the unspeakable horror of what had been done and the indestructible beauty of what remained. Sometimes the world of our experience is maimed by human wickedness—by terrorists or rapists, by dictators or demagogues, by genocidal rulers or homicidal robbers. At other times, our world is mutilated by nature's indifference to our preference for human life over other forms of existence and other forces of nature—by tumors or typhoons, by viruses or volcanoes, by heart attacks or hurricanes. The scars abound everywhere.

Even so, Zagajewski urges, "Try to praise the mutilated world." The word praise comes from the same root as the word price. To praise something is to give it value. Even though the world of our experience has been mutilated, we shouldn't toss it away as worthless or abandon it as rubbish. We should value it despite the maiming—despite what has been cut off or cut out or cut down. Even a mutilated world has intrinsic value.

No matter how damaged, whatever has been mutilated remains an essential part of our experience. The suffering of people everywhere makes up part of the planet we live on: It's our world. In a deep and existential sense, their suffering is part of who we are. To value the mutilated world, therefore, is to value our own experience and our own place. It is also to value the people who have experienced devastating violence and loss. They too have value.

This realization gets to the heart of the role beauty plays in our lives. Beauty, at least in the moral (that is, value-driven) sense, is not a synonym for *attractive* or *pretty*. It's not something that can be created by clothing or enhanced by makeup. Rather, beauty has to do with the nature of the relationships that constitute the world of our experience—with harmony of our relationships and the intensity of their value.

Beauty unfolds when relationships—physical, emotional, or spiritual, among humans or between humans and the rest of the natural world—are harmoniously reciprocal and valuable to everyone and everything involved, both in giving and receiving. On these terms, the purpose of the universe, as Alfred North Whitehead says, is the creation and enjoyment of beauty.

Elaine Scarry, a professor of aesthetics at Harvard, explores the consequences of this understanding of beauty in her book titled *On Beauty and Being Just*. Over the centuries, she says, the attribute most consistently singled out to define beauty has been symmetry: a sense of balance and proportion. She points out that our experiences of beauty establish a standard or an ideal—a benchmark by which we can measure our conduct and our lives.

For this reason, Scarry insists, beauty has built-in consequences. The consequences are best captured in our language by a single word, fairness, which refers both to the attractiveness of a face (the oldest sense of the word *fair* meant pleasant or agreeable, as in fair weather) and to the ethical requirement to be fair, play fair, or distribute fairly. Beauty creates a covenant with people who experience it. It expresses symmetry and reciprocity—not just in music and art, but also in our relations with each other and with our world. In political terms, Scarry says, beauty calls us to justice.

We need to give all we have to create beauty—as harmony, as value, as justice—in whatever form we can, wherever we can, using whatever means we have available. In this endeavor, proximity matters. Even though we live at the center of a vast constellation of relationships that ultimately connect us to everything, we're not responsible to create beauty everywhere. Rather, our gratitude goal is to create beauty wherever *we* are.

THE EARLY-TWENTIETH-CENTURY POET Sara Teasdale celebrates the experience of beauty and the claim these experiences make on us in her poem "Barter." In 1918, Teasdale was awarded the first Columbia Poetry Prize, a prize that would later be renamed the Pulitzer Prize for Poetry. She writes, in part:

> *Life has loveliness to sell,*
> > *All beautiful and splendid things,*
> *Blue waves whitened on a cliff,*
> > *Soaring fire that sways and sings,*
> *And children's faces looking up,*
> *Holding wonder like a cup.*

> *Life has loveliness to sell,*
> > *Music like a curve of gold,*
> *Scent of pine trees in the rain,*
> > *Eyes that love you, arms that hold,*
> *And for your spirit's still delight,*
> *Holy thoughts that star the night.*

The poem concludes with a reminder of what we owe in response: In exchange for all this loveliness, Teasdale urges, "give all you have been, or could be." Life offers us a deal. In gratitude for the loveliness life has "sold" us, we owe a reciprocal commitment as payment in return.

LIFE ALSO HAS many things to sell that aren't lovely. Nonetheless, the experience of beauty continually reminds us that mutilation need not have the final word. Even in the midst of grief and devastation, the lingering presence of beauty in its many forms invites us to envision a world once again made whole.

Marietta Moskin, a longtime member of my congregation who died some years ago, wrote seventeen books for children and young adults. One was a prize-winning novel titled *I Am Rosemarie,* based on her own life as a young girl in Hitler's concentration camps.

After being freed from the camps by the Allies, Rosemarie and her mother, along with a family friend named Kay, did something they hadn't done in years: They bought shoes. They found a shop, selected several pairs, and handed over payment using a bill denominated in marks, the German currency. The bill they handed to the shopkeeper was worth one million marks—a bill that had been used before the war when inflation was running rampant.

The shopkeeper blanched. In the post-war economy,

his entire shop was worth only a fraction of that amount. When the local French commander ordered the shopkeeper to honor the note, the shopkeeper insisted on giving them the shoes at no cost. Otherwise, the only way he could have made change was to give them his shop.

Rosemarie's mother turned to her friend Kay and remarked that she was beginning to feel sorry for the shopkeeper. Moskin writes:

> Kay looked at her scornfully. "I'm surprised at you," she said. "Getting all soft and tenderhearted. You—after all you've been through. Don't you hate the bastards? I do!"
>
> "Hate?" my mother said softly. "I don't really want to hate. It's such a futile emotion. It tears you all up inside—and for what? Do you think any of them will care if we hate them? They'll just laugh at us. Hating hurts no one but yourself! . . ."
>
> My mother was right, I thought. It takes too much effort to hate. It is too painful. I don't want to be angry and bitter and all cold and hard inside. The day is too nice, and the sun is shining and I am walking with lovely new shoes. I am free at last!

The effort to create beauty knows no bounds. There's a lot Rosemarie couldn't control, from the outcome of the Holocaust, to the post-war economy in Germany, to the attitude of the defeated Germans. But she could control her own attitude and attention, and she did. Rather than being angry and bitter, which she had every reason to be, she chose to focus on the beautiful day, the shining sun, and her freedom to walk in her lovely new shoes.

No matter how devastating or discouraging our present circumstances may be, Zagajewski urges us to remember the "wild strawberries, drops of wine, [and] the dew," in order to buoy our spirits until these experiences return. We remember "the moments when we were together," in order to keep our faith strong until we are together once again. We remember "the concert where music flared," in order to remind us that we will eventually hear music once again. We remember "the gentle light that strays and vanishes / and returns," knowing that life sometimes ebbs and flows like the daylight. Remembering, we celebrate the beauty that lingers still, and we give increased value to the beauty we seek to restore.

# CHAPTER 11

# *Gratitude Maximizes Dignity*

ঐ

To sin by silence, when we should protest,
Makes cowards out of men. The human race
Has climbed on protest. Had no voice been raised
Against injustice, ignorance, and lust,
The inquisition yet would serve the law,
And guillotines decide our least disputes.
The few who dare, must speak and speak again
To right the wrongs of many. . . .

Therefore I do protest against the boast
Of independence in this mighty land.
Call no chain strong, which holds one rusted link.
Call no land free, that holds one fettered slave.
Until the manacled slim wrists of babes
Are loosed to toss in childish sport and glee,
Until the mother bears no burden, save
The precious one beneath her heart, until
God's soil is rescued from the clutch of greed
And given back to labor, let no man
Call this the land of freedom.

ELLA WHEELER WILCOX (1850–1919),
EXCERPT FROM "PROTEST"

MY FATHER GREW up in the far reaches of upstate New York, a stone's throw from Lake Ontario and twenty miles or so from Canada. During the winter, icy air sweeping south from the Arctic met moisture moving east across the lake. Especially during the Great Depression, when my grandparents struggled to provide food even for their own family, roving strangers then known as tramps would regularly show up at the door. All of them were hungry, and some of them had tuberculosis, which apparently was rampant. My grandmother always fed them, even if it meant she had less for her own family, and even if she had to go without food herself. She sometimes also had to throw away the plates and utensils to protect herself and her family from disease. "We should always be ready to help people in need," my grandmother said.

Her commitment served as an informal Mennonite motto: *Always be ready to help people in need.* When natural disasters strike, Mennonite Disaster Service deploys Mennonite volunteers from across the country—carpenters, masons, plumbers, and electricians, among other trades—to help stricken communities rebuild. Mennonite Central Committee sends relief workers and supplies to communities around the world suffering from calamities caused either by nature or by human nature. It's an impressive legacy of humanitarian service.

When it came to government policies that may cause or exacerbate human suffering, however, the Conservative Mennonites of my upbringing took a different approach. They understood themselves to be the quiet in the land, limiting their involvement in the political arena to "rendering unto Caesar his due" by paying taxes. Like their better-known relatives, the Amish, the Conservative Mennonites believe God has set them apart from those whose lives focus on worldly concerns, including politics. They do not fight in wars, nor do they vote for politicians, who may decide to send our nation to war. My expectation growing up was that I would never vote, as my parents to this day have never voted.

Over time, I realized that this cloistered approach wouldn't work for me. On October 7, 1988, the *Chicago Tribune* published my op-ed column describing why I registered to vote for the first time at the age of thirty. I was a PhD student at the University of Chicago at the time. Almost on a whim, I filled out the form and took the oath at the student center while on coffee break from studying in the library. But my decision had been years in the making.

In the *Tribune* column, I said, "Many of my parents' answers have not worked so well in my world. In forging new ways of living and thinking, I have transgressed the boundary between the church and the world. The symbolic wall between the first and the third person plural has collapsed. In many ways, I stand on the outside of the church, looking in. Registering to vote confirms this movement to the boundary."

Once beyond the boundary, I came to realize in a new way what is required to help people in need, especially those in greatest need. We first acknowledge our good fortune: the gifts that life has bestowed on us, whether they came to us unbidden or because of our hard work and perseverance. Even if we aren't the most fortunate people we know, and none of us are, we are also not the least fortunate people we know. Our basic desires in life mirror those of other people, none of whom are inherently less deserving—or more deserving—than we are. Our gratitude goal should be to maximize human dignity: the value and potential of each human life.

If people who have fallen by the wayside are to achieve their full potential, however, there must be a political dimension to establishing their rights and ensuring their dignity. As Ella Wheeler Wilcox puts it in her ferocious poem that opens this chapter, "The human race / Has climbed on protest." If no voice had been raised over the years against injustice, ignorance, and lust, she says, "The inquisition yet would serve the law, / And guillotines decide our least disputes." From the Civil War and the women's suffrage movement of the nineteenth century, to the civil rights and gay rights movements of the twentieth century, to Occupy Wall

Street and #MeToo movements in the twenty-first century, among many others, progress in our nation has always been signposted by protest. The difference has been made by "the few who dare," those who "speak and speak again to right the wrongs of many."

ONE OF THE most determined advocates to undertake this political task has been Eleanor Roosevelt, who chaired a UN subcommittee that was charged with developing a Universal Declaration of Human Rights (UDHR) in the aftermath of the humanitarian horrors of two world wars. Roosevelt relentlessly pursued a declaration that would champion not just human rights in the narrow sense, but human dignity in the broadest sense.

On December 10, 1948, delegates to the fledgling United Nations adopted the UDHR. As the delegates contemplated the inhumane brutality the first half of the twentieth century had produced, they put in place a new slate of standards, based on their commitment to extend to all human beings the full equality of human rights and human dignity. Among other things, the delegates declared:

> All human beings are born free and equal in dignity and rights. They are endowed with reason and conscience and should act

towards one another in a spirit of good-will. . . . Everyone has the right to life, liberty, and security of person. . . . No one should be subjected to torture or to cruel, inhuman or degrading treatment or punishment. . . . Everyone has the right to freedom of thought, conscience and religion. . . . Everyone has the right to take part in the government of his or her country, directly or through freely chosen representation. Everyone has the right to marry and found a family. . . . Everyone has the right to work, to free choice of employment, to just and favorable conditions of work . . . the right to rest and leisure . . . the right to a standard of living adequate for the health and well-being of themselves and their family . . . the right to education.

And so on. The assumption underlying this declaration is that individual citizens have access to the opportunities that these freedoms describe. In order for you to have free choice of employment, for example, jobs need to be available for which you are trained and qualified—and they need to be jobs you're interested in doing and would enable you to earn a living.

Martha Nussbaum, a philosopher and legal scholar at the University of Chicago, insists that freedom and equality are more elusive than we think. In her book *Frontiers of Justice,* she says that if we are fortunate, the assumption that we are "free, equal, and independent" is true for at least part of our lives. But it is never true for any of us throughout all of life. Babies are not free, equal, and independent; nor are many people who are elderly. Nor are we if we become sick or disabled, or if we are born poor or disadvantaged in some other way. Since being free and independent is at best a temporary condition, Nussbaum argues that we should think of human rights not only in terms of freedom, but also in terms of what she calls capabilities.

The question, in her view, isn't only whether you are free to have clean water, but also whether you are at least minimally capable of getting it. Are you minimally capable of finding shelter or medical care; of using your senses to imagine, think, and reason; of participating in the political choices that govern your life; of acquiring and holding property? Nussbaum's point is that the right to something is worthless without at least a minimal capability of exercising that right.

What are the odds of any one of us being born with a full set of rights and the capabilities to exercise them? The odds are abysmal. If you're not starving for food, if you're not worried that someone's going to take you captive or steal your possessions, and if you have time to read a book and resources to buy one, you are one of the most fortunate people in human history.

This good fortune isn't of your own doing. None of us has any control over the circumstances of our birth, the capabilities we bring into the world, or the potential of the context in which we grow up. In this respect, life isn't fair. Some people, through no merit of their own, were born to vastly more possibilities than others. Roughly half of the world's population has been born male, and virtually every human culture, including today's most advanced cultures, has privileged men over women, who have been oppressed in myriad ways. In most Western cultures, light-skinned people of European heritage have typically found themselves privileged over darker-skinned people, who have also been oppressed in myriad ways.

Beyond gender and race, other characteristics give certain people a built-in advantage. Some individuals have more talents (or talents that are more highly valued) than other people. They may be stronger or viewed as more attractive. They may also have been born with—or trained to embody—sufficient diligence and discipline to make good on their early promise. Their parents may have above-average financial resources, giving them access to high-quality medical care and educational environments.

If we acknowledge that the circumstances of our birth are determined by sheer chance, then we should also acknowledge that the happenstance of birth should not ultimately define the possibilities of life. People who suffer oppression from the start aren't any less deserving than those of us who had a fulsome start. Trying to make good on good fortune also entails trying to help people make good on bad fortune.

The problem is that many of the social and political structures in place today were designed to predetermine a good outcome—but only for certain kinds of people. When Congress adopted the Declaration of Independence in 1776, the signers of the Declaration explicitly viewed equality not only as gender-specific (it applied only to men), but also as race-specific (it applied only to men of European descent). It would be nearly one hundred years until non-white men and freed male slaves were granted the right to vote in 1870 and nearly one hundred and fifty years until women were granted the right to vote in 1920.

In 1969, the Norwegian sociologist and mathematician Johan Galtung coined the term "structural violence" to describe how the structure of society itself can prevent certain people from meeting their basic needs, thereby causing undue hardship and suffering. In the United States, such structures—including laws, policies, and institutions—were explicitly put in place from the outset to privilege men over women, white Europeans over people of color, Protestants over adherents to other faiths, and straight people over LGBTQ people. Many of our nation's fiercest battles have been fought in an effort to make right these founding wrongs.

During the time Jonathan Sacks was the Chief Rabbi of Great Britain, he wrote *The Dignity of Difference: How to Avoid the Clash of Civilization*. He observes that economic superpowers, which may seem invincible in their time, have a relatively short life span: Venice in the sixteenth century, the Netherlands in the seventeenth, France in the eighteenth, Britain in the nineteenth, and the United States in the twentieth. The great religions, by contrast, have been able to survive: Islam for 1,500 years, Christianity for 2,000 years, and Judaism for 4,000 years.

Why is this so? These faith traditions, Sacks says, "remind us that civilizations survive not by strength but by how they respond to the weak; not by wealth but by the care they show for the poor; not by power but by their concern for the powerless. The ironic yet utterly humane lesson of history is that what renders a culture invulnerable is the compassion it shows to the vulnerable. The ultimate value we should be concerned to maximize is human dignity—the dignity of all human beings, equally, as children of the creative, redeeming God."

As Sacks notes, the religious mandate to maximize dignity is clear. According to the Hebrew prophet Micah, the essence of the Jewish faith is simply this: Act justly, love mercy, and walk humbly with your God. The Christian New Testament is equally explicit. When Jesus was asked to identify the greatest commandment in the law, he replied, "Love God, and love your neigh-bor." He told the story of the Good Samaritan to illus-trate that the people who will be greatest in the kingdom of God are those who help people in need. In a similar way, the third pillar of Islam, Zakat, calls for the purifi-cation of wealth by giving a portion of it to those who are in need.

The lesson of history is that no political or economic system based on human freedom can survive if the dig-nity and rights of some people are marginalized, trivial-ized, or invalidated. As Ella Wheeler Wilcox says, no chain is strong that holds one rusted link. No land is free that holds one fettered slave. We can't call our land the land of freedom until everyone is free.

JOHN RAWLS, THE late Harvard political philosopher, says that we can only develop good public policy from behind what he calls a veil of ignorance. When we are behind this veil, Rawls says, we do not know who ex-actly we are in society, or what position we hold, nor do we have any specific knowledge of our life's goals and plans. To think about what is right, we have to assume that we could be anyone, and that the odds are not nec-essarily in our favor. Put another way, if I do not know beforehand which piece of cake I will end up with, then I will do my best to divide the cake fairly.

Our economic system is built on the premise that

people are free to work hard and get ahead, which means securing a bigger piece of cake. Rawls doesn't say everyone's piece of cake must be the same size, only that changes in public policy should not reduce the size of the smallest pieces or reduce the chance that people with small pieces can find ways to get bigger ones. Changes in public policy must enhance, and not diminish, the prospects of the least well off.

In addition to working to make our public policies fair for everyone, we also need to help people who are in need, as my grandmother did. If someone is in distress and we can help, then we should help. If we see a positive difference that we could make, then we should make it. In gratitude for what we have been given in life, we respond by maximizing human dignity wherever we can.

JEFFRO BRYANT WAS an affable and elderly man who served as a custodian at All Souls for a number of years until his death. Jeffro first came to All Souls as a guest at our Friday Soup kitchen. Friday Soup, along with Monday Night Hospitality, are weekly volunteer-led programs that serve dinner on Monday and lunch on Friday to our homeless neighbors and others who need sustenance. Over the course of a year, we serve upward of forty thousand meals. The guests are served family style at round tables adorned with tablecloths, flower centerpieces, and place settings. The waiters and kitchen staff are all volunteers—fifty or more per meal.

When I can, I help out at Monday Night Hospitality, usually by greeting guests who are waiting in line to enter Reidy Friendship Hall. We offer them coffee, along with hot chocolate in cold weather and iced tea when it's warm. I also greet the volunteers before table service begins and offer them a brief word of thanks. I usually say that our guests' need for food brings them in the door, but the sense of human dignity that they receive at dinner keeps them coming back.

Week after week, Jeffro kept coming back to Friday Soup, commuting from the homeless shelter where he lived. Gradually, he began helping out around the church in various ways, and eventually he became a full-time member of the All Souls staff. We helped Jeffro find a subsidized apartment near the church, and then he was able to buy a big flat-screen television, which had a place of pride in his apartment.

Many early mornings when I was the only person yet to have arrived in the church offices, Jeffro would come by to collect the trash, and we'd chat—just the two of us. We'd debate the relative merits of Alabama, where he grew up, and Arkansas, where I did. He'd ask how the All Souls at Sundown jazz and poetry service had gone or how my daughter, Zoë, was doing. I'd ask about his weekend—what games he'd watched on his television and how much he had won in the lottery. Whenever I was travelling for a few days, he'd ask where I went and what I did.

Jeffro seemed especially proud that I had finally received my PhD, knowing that it had taken me seventeen years to complete the degree. When I returned from the commencement ceremony in Chicago, he asked to see the pictures and looked carefully at each one. Ever after, he called me Dr. Galen—one of the only people at All Souls to do so.

One morning as Jeffro and I met in passing, we exchanged greetings, and then I asked him how his day was going. "It's too early to tell, Dr. Galen. It's too early to tell." By then, we had passed each other, but Jeffro stopped and called after me: "You know, Dr. Galen, that would make a good sermon title some Sunday morning, don't you think? 'Too early to tell'?"

I readily agreed that it would and told him I'd keep it in mind. Then we both went off to our work. Several years later, I used the title on the Sunday morning after Jeffro died.

I loved Jeffro's laconic enthusiasm for life, and I miss him still. When I'm in my office in the early morning and hear the outer door open, I sometimes still expect to hear Jeffro say, "Morning, Dr. Galen." In the ways that matter most, I like to think that we helped save Jeffro's life—and that he helped save our lives as well.

There's no joy sweeter than knowing that we've helped someone find a source of value.

Each of us has a crucial role to play, no matter who or where we are. In gratitude for the freedom and capabilities we have been given, we should do whatever we can to maximize human dignity, one person at a time.

# CHAPTER 12

# *Gratitude Seeks Possibility*

ટ્

I dwell in Possibility –
A fairer House than Prose –
More numerous of Windows –
Superior – for Doors –

Of Chambers as the Cedars –
Impregnable of eye –
And for an everlasting Roof
The Gambrels of the Sky –

Of Visitors – the fairest –
For Occupation – This –
The spreading wide my narrow Hands
To gather Paradise –

EMILY DICKINSON (1830–1886)

ONE OF THE most compelling stories in the Hebrew Bible, and also one of the most disturbing, appears in Genesis 22. God tests the patriarch Abraham by asking him to journey with his son Isaac to a mountain several days away, where he is to slay his son Isaac and offer him as a burnt sacrifice. As Abraham and Isaac make the journey, a recurring and internally repetitive line in the story heightens the sense of what is at risk: "The two of them walked on together." Fortunately for Isaac, an angel aborts this divine test of allegiance at the last minute, and Abraham finds a ram caught in a thicket nearby to place on the altar as a substitute. The artists Titian, Caravaggio, Rembrandt, and Chagall, among many others, depict this story at its moment of highest tension.

Despite the drama, I find the idea of God asking Abraham to kill his child abhorrent. A God who makes such demands is not a God I can believe in. The story does, however, powerfully make its point: Abraham's confidence in God is unshakable.

En route, Isaac asks his father, "We have the wood and the fire for the burnt offering, but where is the lamb?" Abraham replies, "God will provide the lamb for the burnt offering, my son." Abraham's ambiguous reply doesn't make clear whether "my son" is the person to whom he's speaking, the lamb God has provided, or both. But it does make clear who is responsible: "God will provide."

As I read this story growing up, studied it in Sunday school, and eventually memorized it, the point got hammered home: "God will provide." Writ large, this response cedes the territory of the future entirely to divine control. In New Testament terms, "All things work together for good to them that love God."

Except that sometimes God doesn't provide. Sometimes things don't work together for good. Whether the issue is the suffering of innocents or the triumph of tyranny, among countless other travesties of human history, the evidence suggests that the future is not under divine control.

But if God doesn't control the future, then who or what does? Some people today, especially those who reject any notion of the divine, believe that only physical entities exist. In such a world, every event would be completely governed by the laws of cause and effect—directly and physically determined by what had happened before. In principle, if we had a big enough computer to track the infinite number of subatomic particles that make up the physical world, we could predict everything that will happen between now and the end of time. All events would thus be necessary events.

This view of the world, known as determinism, closely parallels the view of classical theologians, who view the world as governed by God's perfect knowledge of the future. Instead of cause and effect determining all future events, God ultimately controls everything that will happen. In either case, whether the world is wholly determined by cause and effect or wholly controlled by a supernatural God, there would, at any given moment, be only one possible future.

Truth be told, even if our future as human beings has been preordained by divine decree, we don't know what the decree foretells. And even if our future has been preordained by the configuration of subatomic particles, we don't know what that future might be either. As far as we know, even though the story of the past cannot be changed, the story of the future has yet to be told.

For its part, science prefers possibility. The physicist Brian Greene explains that quantum theory portrays reality as a haze of possibilities, especially at the subatomic level, because no one knows where a given particle will be at a given time. For an electron circling the nucleus of an atom, for example, there's a 13 percent chance that an electron will be here, and a 19 percent chance that it will be there. As objects become larger, they become much more predictable. But at the fundamental level, the best we can do is talk about possible outcomes. Greene says, "When we make a measurement or perform an observation, we force the myriad possibilities to . . . snap out of the haze and settle on a single outcome. But between observations—when we're not looking—reality consists entirely of jostling possibilities."

When we look at reality from a spiritual perspective, we also find a preference for possibility. As I noted in chapter six, Alfred North Whitehead insists that just as atoms are never lost in physical reactions, so no human experience is ever eternally forgotten. Once something has happened, it remains forever part of the experiences that make up existence as we understand it. As White-

head puts it, everything that happens in the universe—
"its sufferings, its sorrows, its triumphs, its immediacies
of joy"—is woven into the harmony of a completed
whole.

This is Whitehead's way of describing spiritual experience at its most comprehensive and most profound. I
describe it as the ultimate spiritual experience. It's the
experience of being deeply connected to everything: all
that is present in our life and our world, and all that is
past and all that is possible. When I use the term God,
which I occasionally do, I do so in this sense—as the
experience of ultimate belonging.

There's another reason to understand spiritual experience at its most capacious as divine, which has to do
with the future. At any given moment, the future can
unfold in a number of possible ways. These possibilities
must come from somewhere. Identifying the source of
possibilities turns out to be a knotty philosophical
problem, as does the presence of possibilities that "exist"
for a time but don't get realized.

For his part, Whitehead views the experience of possibility as the forward-looking aspect of feeling deeply
connected to everything. Just as he views the ultimate
refuge of all past experiences as divine, he also views the
transcendent source of all future possibilities as divine.
He describes this divine source as "the eternal urge of
desire." It accounts for our sense that the future can
unfold in a purposive and meaningful way, even though

it sometimes doesn't. This experience, Whitehead says, opens up "a vision of truth, beauty, and goodness."

People sometimes ask me how I understand the role of the divine in this world, given that I don't believe in God in the traditional sense. My response is a simple one: *God is the experience of possibility.* What could be more divine than a future open to creative advance?

If I were banished to a desert isle and could take only one volume of poetry with me, I would take Emily Dickinson's collected poems. She's my favorite poet, in part because she has penned my favorite line of poetry:

> *I dwell in Possibility –*

The poem concludes:

> *For Occupation – This –*
> *The spreading wide my narrow Hands*
> *To gather Paradise –*

Our true occupation as human beings on this earth is to open our arms in gratitude for all that is past and all that is possible—to gather paradise, in Dickinson's turn of phrase.

VIEWED IN SPIRITUAL terms, our gratitude for the gift of each moment gives hope that the future will unfold in a way that tends toward meaning and not toward chaos. When the ancient Greeks pondered the future, they often spoke of the tendency of the future to move toward a particular goal, like the tendency of a plant to grow toward the sun. The plant can be temporarily turned away, of course, but it will always grow back toward the light.

When we live with gratitude, our goal is not to replicate the past, but to imagine the future. For its part, the past provides the raw materials: the circumstances of our birth, our talents, our educational achievements, our failures in love, our successes at work, and so on. We have everything that is past to work with—and nothing more.

Within these constraints, we have a certain amount of freedom—sometimes more, sometimes less—to determine how we construct our future. Those of us who practice gratitude as a way of life practice the art of the possible. Our gratitude goal should be to advance the potential of the future. Look at what is and imagine what could be. Look at brokenness and envision what healing would look like. Look at hatred and envision what love would look like. Look at failure and envision what success would look like.

At least in this universe, the work of forging the future, of turning toward the light, will not be done by subatomic particles alone. Nor will it be done by divine decrees. Rather, it will be done by human beings—by you and me. From our point of view, you and I live at the intersection of necessity and possibility. It's the place where, and the moment when, all that is past meets all that is possible.

It's true that the future—our future and the world's future—will continue to arrive even if we do nothing. In this case, the future will continue mostly to mirror the past, and nothing much will ever turn out differently. If there is such a thing as sin in a life of gratitude, the decision to do nothing would be its essence. In its original meaning, the word *sin* derived from an ancient archery term used to describe an arrow that had missed its mark and the effort of the archer who had shot it. To sin is to miss the mark—to allow all that is possible to collapse into all that is past.

The human story, therefore, is the story of agency. We are agents of possibility, whereby necessity engages possibility and the past becomes the future. This puts us in a position of daunting—even unbelievable—influence. Because of our choices and actions, human history will forever be different, even if the difference initially appears inconsequential. But small changes add up over time and, when multiplied by the efforts of others, can eventually make a transformative difference.

ONE OF THE greatest prophets of possibility in the twentieth century was Dr. Martin Luther King Jr. In his speeches and writings, he acknowledged our nation's deep connection to its slavery-based past and its segregation-saturated present. He witnessed the active violence of Southern whites against their black neighbors, as well as the structural violence present throughout the nation in unequal access to education, housing, and other essential opportunities. But he rejected the idea that the horrors of the past and the troubles of the present had spoken the final word. Despite the chasm between our nation's lofty words and its often-destructive deeds, Dr. King saw the possibilities represented by our nation's professed ideal of freedom.

Echoing the biblical story of Moses, who led the children of Israel out of slavery in Egypt, Dr. King declared: "I have been to the mountaintop, and I have seen the Promised Land." The possibilities he saw there gave him hope. I have a dream, he proclaimed, that our nation will one day live up to its founding creed of equality. I have a dream, he continued, that "my four little children will one day live in a nation where they will not be judged by the color of their skin but by the content of their character." Go back home, Dr. King counseled his listeners, "knowing that somehow this situation can and will be changed. Let us not wallow in the valley of despair."

No matter how trying the past has been, nor how difficult the present, our current circumstances need not have the final word. Today is another day. Even if you gave in to temptation yesterday, failed to follow through on a commitment, or disappointed yourself or someone you love, today is another day. Within the limits set by the circumstances you find yourself in and the resources you can bring to bear, anything is possible.

The important task, as Emily Dickinson emphasizes at the beginning of her poem, is to dwell in possibility—dwell in it. Today, you have another chance. Be relentless in your pursuit of whatever is possible. Advance the potential of the future in every way you can. Don't be seduced into continually revisiting the past, saying, "If only . . ." Don't be seduced into wistfully imagining the future, saying, "I wish . . ." Instead, dwell in possibility. Ask yourself what you can do now to advance the potential of the future.

What could be better? To be able to live another moment, even another day, is a gift beyond measure. As we live in gratitude for this gift, we open our arms wide to the possibilities that lie before us.

ॐ

## PART THREE

*The Practice of Gratitude*

# CHAPTER 13

# Gratitude as Spiritual Practice

In the name of the daybreak
and the eyelids of morning
and the wayfaring moon
and the night when it departs,

I swear I will not dishonor
my soul with hatred,
but offer myself humbly
as a guardian of nature,
as a healer of misery,
as a messenger of wonder,
as an architect of peace.

In the name of the sun and its mirrors
and the day that embraces it
and the cloud veils drawn over it
and the uttermost night
and the male and the female
and the plants bursting with seed
and the crowning seasons
of the firefly and the apple,

I will honor all life
—wherever and in whatever form
it may dwell—on Earth my home,
and in the mansions of the stars.

DIANE ACKERMAN (B. 1948), "SCHOOL PRAYER"

DURING THE YEARLONG Coming of Age curriculum for ninth graders at All Souls, teens are asked to describe any rituals they have at home. One year, a young woman I'll call Maggie said that her family recites a particular prayer every evening before dinner. As soon as Maggie was old enough to memorize the prayer, she and her older sister used to argue over who got to say it each night. At some point, her sister decided she didn't believe what the prayer said, so Maggie got to say it every night.

The time came when Maggie decided that the words of the prayer didn't suit her either. But she didn't stop saying the prayer; she rewrote it. Maggie said that one of the things she likes about her prayer is that it helps those who hear it remember that if they have food on their table, they are privileged. It reminds them to be grateful.

For Maggie's family, prayer before dinner, whether in its original form or a revised version, keeps them from forgetting what must not be forgotten. The specific words didn't matter all that much. What matters is the reminder to pause and be grateful. Philip Rieff, a leading social theorist in the late twentieth century who didn't believe in God, once quipped, "The family who prays together stays together, whether there is a god or not."

When Zoë was six or seven years old, she decided that Holly and I should say a blessing to her each night as she went to bed. She got the idea from a book for children of divorced parents titled *It's Not Your Fault, Koko Bear*. The blessing Zoë wanted us to say was this: "You are the Zoë for whom we care. You are so blessed: none can compare."

What's the point of these few simple words? When Holly and I tucked Zoë into bed at night, we didn't know all of the things she had experienced that day. Maybe her teacher was brusque with her. Maybe she got pushed down on the playground during recess. Maybe one of her friends wouldn't sit with her at lunchtime. Whatever happened, she knew that at the end of the day, she would hear these few words. Rituals help restore our sense of safety and security.

Rituals also remind us of what is important. In the hustle and bustle of our daily lives, we mostly focus on what's urgent, sometimes at the expense of what's ultimately important. Our most urgent priorities each day are typically set by our longest-standing commitments, whether to our family members, to work, or to friends. If we need to take a child to the doctor, finish a report, get the car serviced, or celebrate a birthday, we dutifully—and rightly—attend to these responsibilities. As we react to urgent demands on our attention, our spiritual lives tend to slip into the background. We don't take time to renew our awareness of the many gifts each day bestows on us and what we owe in response.

For these reasons and others, we need to bring our spiritual life into the foreground—not once in a while, but every day. We can accomplish this through what I have come to call the First Light Meditation. In my experience, this spiritual practice helps recalibrate my awareness each morning, thus helping ensure that the day's journey will take me in the right spiritual direction. I invite you to give it a try.

As outlined here, the First Light Meditation takes less than fifteen minutes to complete each morning. If that's too long at first, or if you find yourself squeezed for time some mornings, you can shorten the meditation significantly. Even taking five minutes to collect yourself and think about your aspirations for the day will make a significant difference in your overall equilibrium. Gratitude as a spiritual practice can also involve a weekly media fast and a monthly food fast, both of which I will outline as well.

Taken together, these daily, weekly, and monthly practices can help us keep our most important commitments front and center in our lives. Among other things, a spiritual practice is a practice: something that's intended to be done repeatedly over a long period of time. Like learning to play the piano beautifully, it takes practice to develop a way of life that's spiritually grounded. Gratitude as a spiritual practice can help move us toward that goal.

Our journey each day along the way of gratitude begins with a step in the right direction. After all, if we don't know where we are going, we're almost certain to end up somewhere random. Once we have a clear goal in mind, we can more easily follow the path that will lead us there.

The way of gratitude begins anew each day at first light. Our eyes may open in the lingering dark, or the day may already be fully bright. Either way, the time to set our spiritual compass for the day comes during those precious moments before the myriad demands of the day seize our attention.

At first light, we have an opportunity to recall our commitments and set our intention for the day's journey. It's true that how we spend any one day may not seem to matter all that much, at least when set against the backdrop of a lifetime of days. But days are not a renewable resource. Each day we pass aimlessly leaves one less day on course. And none of us knows when our individual supply of days will run out. The only days we are guaranteed are the ones we have—this one and those that came before. We respond at first light to the gift of another day by taking time to make gratitude our spiritual practice.

The practice at first light has three simple elements: pause, ponder, and pray. You can do the practice anywhere—wherever you can find a quiet place to be alone before the day begins. You will need a candle and something to light it, along with a one-page-per-day journal and a three-minute sand timer. Ideally, these should be not just functional items, but beautiful as well. They will be present with you during the most important part of your day.

Begin by lighting the candle, which symbolizes three things: the light of the new day, the illumination you will receive during your practice, and the energy that will sustain you throughout the day. Then pause; for a few minutes, simply pay attention to yourself—the breath that fills your lungs, the blood coursing through your arteries and veins, the weight of your body upon the earth, the sense of space that surrounds you. Use the sand timer to pace your pause. The falling sand is a good reminder that each moment is irretrievable and therefore precious.

As your pause comes to an end, turn the timer over for another three minutes. Then let your mind drift to the events of yesterday. Think about whatever's past that you need to leave behind—a disappointment, perhaps, or maybe a commitment you didn't keep. Then shift your focus to the present moment—what you're concerned about, what you need, maybe even what you fear. And finally, open your mind to the day that has just dawned—think about what's possible. What attitude do you most want to maintain, or which task do you most want to accomplish? Take time to write down the three things you have just named: what you have left in the past, what you have named in the present, and what you have claimed for the future. The arc of gratitude always moves from what's past, through what's present, and toward what's possible.

Next, ponder the First Light Meditation. You will find a starter collection of meditations in Appendix B of this book. You can access ongoing meditations at galenguengerich.com, where you will find meditations for each day going forward. You can also sign up to have the meditations emailed to you. In this way, you will keep company, at least in spirit, with spiritual seekers across the country and even around the world who ponder the same passage on the same day.

Turning the timer again, read the meditation several times, preferably aloud, each time placing emphasis on different words and phrases. As you read, reflect on what the meditation means. What response does it provoke? What does it say to you—to you in particular—about the day ahead? As you turn the timer a final time, write down your thoughts and reactions in your journal.

The third step in the practice at first light is to pray. In this context, prayer is not the process of articulating things you want, as though you were preparing a list for a cosmic delivery service. Rather, prayer is the process of declaring what you most deeply desire for yourself and your world. In prayer, you focus your intention for the day ahead.

Slowly and meditatively, read these words aloud:

> *I receive the gift of this day with gratitude.*
> *I seek to accept all that is past.*
> *I seek to embrace all that is present.*
> *I seek to realize all that is possible:*
> > *the clarity of truth,*
> > *the joy of beauty,*
> > *the satisfaction of justice,*
> > *the lure of adventure,*
> > *the fullness of peace.*
> *I seek to be worthy of the gift of this day.*

As you end your prayer, focus on your gratitude for the past that has formed you, the present that now holds you, and the future that beckons you. Today is a one-time-only gift. You will not pass this way again.

Then extinguish the flame. You are now ready to begin your day—the first day of the rest of your life.

FIRST DAY FAST

As a spiritual practice, gratitude aligns our daily attitudes and choices with our commitments and aspirations. The two First Day practices accomplish these goals by interrupting, albeit briefly, our usual patterns of interaction. I recommend forgoing email and social media, as well as television and movies, one day a week—a digital fast. I recommend refraining from eating food one day a month—a traditional fast. The daylong digital fast each week reminds us to reconnect in real ways with the people around us and with the natural world. The daylong traditional fast each month reminds us of our dependence on the natural world for our sustenance. Taken together, these practices reinforce our commitment to gratitude as a way of life.

Of the two, the weekly digital fast is probably the more difficult for most of us to accomplish. The smartphone—and its tablet, laptop, and desktop equivalents—has become the hearthstone of the modern world, or perhaps its village square. Increasingly, these devices are where we spend our time—doing our work, connecting with other people, and entertaining ourselves.

Unlike hearthstones and village squares, however, smartphones and other digital devices bring people together by enabling them to stay apart, leading to increasingly impersonal modes of human communication. Gratitude requires openness, and technology has proven to be an effective means of closing ourselves off. For this reason, it is a good idea to turn off our digital devices once in a while. I have found once a week to be a viable pattern, and I like the symbolism of the first day of the week. In this way, we remind ourselves of the commitments that have first priority in our lives.

Under ideal circumstances, the daylong digital fast would extend throughout the day—from before we awaken in the morning until after we go to sleep at night. Fortunately, most of our digital devices can be programmed to conform to this pattern. However, given our contemporary approaches to work and parenting, along with other demands on our time, we may find this approach unworkable. Given my own commitments as a preacher and pastor on Sundays, for example, I typically need to reconfigure my fast. If you find yourself needing to do the same, here's my recommendation: Either move your digital fast to a different day or extend your fast as long as possible on Sundays. I try to make it at least eight hours in any case.

Remember that the digital fast isn't an end in itself, but rather serves a spiritual purpose. Each of us is made up of a unique set of relationships. Friends, colleagues, classmates, immediate family, intimate partners: Our experience of these people and others makes us who we are. By maintaining a digital fast, we set aside time to experience them in person, face-to-face.

The same is true of our experience of the natural world. As we walk along a woodland trail, the sun on our skin, the breeze in our face, and the leaves under our feet give us a sense of being deeply grounded— a sense that photos or videos of the trail could never accomplish. Especially for those of us who spend most of our time in built environments surrounded by inanimate objects, we need to create opportunities to spend time in the living part of the natural world. These experiences help us remember that we are part of a larger living ecosystem.

NOT ONLY ARE we part of the natural world, it is also part of us. We depend on the natural world for our sustenance. In order to remind ourselves of this fundamental reality, I suggest refraining from eating food one day each month—perhaps the first day of the month. For people in reasonably good health, a regular pattern of fasting can be a valuable practice even beyond its spiritual benefits. Before undertaking a fast, you should check with your doctor.

Ideally, the fast should last twenty-four hours—from after dinner one evening until dinner the following evening, or from after breakfast in the morning until breakfast the following morning. In either case, the fast should occupy the daytime hours. As pangs of hunger become more prominent throughout the day, we remember how much we enjoy eating—and how much we need to eat. We also remember not to take for granted the plants and animals that become food for us.

Be sure to drink plenty of fluids during your fast, and break your fast slowly. Again, be sure to check with your doctor, who can offer specific guidance concerning what to drink during your fast and how to break it.

As spiritual seekers have discovered for thousands of years, fasting can be a clarifying and ultimately exhilarating spiritual experience. It can also focus our attention on people around the world for whom hunger remains a persistent reality. Some people today, both in the United States and in nations around the world, struggle to avoid starvation. If they go without food, they do so because they have no choice.

Most of us in developed nations have the opposite problem. We struggle to avoid obesity in a world of food abundance. By fasting, we make common cause with people who live hungry, if only for a day. We also renew our resolve to help make the world a place where everyone has what they need.

A REGULAR PATTERN of fasting, in both its digital and traditional forms, has one further benefit. It increases our sense of discipline—our ability to be firmly in control of our appetites and our actions. Because this ability also benefits other areas of our lives, it's worth developing for its own sake.

As spiritual practices, the First Light Meditation, along with the digital and food fasts, help develop the fitness to carry our practice of gratitude through the rest of our lives. The goal is for gratitude to become not only a spiritual practice, but also a way of life.

# CHAPTER 14

# *Only Forward*

ॐ

It's only life that's the problem,
Life, the famous intricate miracle
That daily converts a crowd of unbelievers.
So many options and still it can't be maneuvered
To take me in any direction except one.
Only one, hour after hour.
Only forward.

CARL DENNIS (B. 1939),
EXCERPT FROM "SWINDLE"

BY THE TIME I was twenty-one, I had made substantial progress in assembling the various elements of a successful life as a Mennonite—and even as a Mennonite minister. After a three-year hiatus between my freshman and sophomore years in college, I was once again back in school, bound eventually for seminary. I was working half-time as a youth minister in a Mennonite church, a role that transitioned into interim pastor when my uncle, who had been pastor of the congregation, abruptly resigned. I was getting married to the eldest daughter of one of the leading families of the congregation. From my perspective at the time, it seemed like a perfect life plan.

Soon thereafter, a member of the congregation invited me to lunch. Doc Herr, as he was known, along with his wife, Lois, had the most cosmopolitan perspective of anyone in the congregation, probably by a wide margin. Located in a rural Mennonite and Amish farming community in Lancaster County, Pennsylvania, the congregation was made up mostly of farmers and people in farm-related trades, along with other blue-collar workers. Doc and Lois had seen the world, and they knew something about its ways.

In particular, they knew how significantly the world of my experience differed from the world I didn't yet know about. Doc's purpose in taking me to lunch was to deliver a simple message that seemed enigmatic to me at the time. He told me that I had a lot of talent and a lot of potential, and he fully expected that I would go on and achieve some things well beyond the scope of the life I currently had in mind.

"There will come a time in your life," he said, "when some of the decisions you have already made for yourself won't make sense anymore. When that time comes, I want you to know that it will be okay for you to revisit those decisions."

He added, "I don't know when that time will come or which decisions you will need to revisit, but I want you to be ready when the time comes."

Doc Herr was right: The time did come. Thanks in

part to him and Lois, I was ready. I knew what I had to do.

As I strode deeper and deeper into the world over the years, it took time for me to recognize my life as genuinely my own. I have tried to stay open to what life has to teach me. I have discovered that living with gratitude, even when life is hard, gives me a deep sense of belonging and a clear sense of purpose. For me, the way of gratitude provides a framework for making decisions about how to live and a set of gratitude goals to guide my efforts to advance the potential of the future.

Sometimes we falter and lose our way, perhaps even fall down. Here's the good news: The way of gratitude always gives us another chance. While we can never revise what's past, the present always brings us another opportunity to seize what's possible. We can forgive ourselves and others—not by papering over our failures in the past or their consequences in the present, but by living differently in the future. The problems of the past can only be redeemed by our actions in the future.

Along the way, we glean new knowledge about ourselves and gain new insights into our world. We develop new relationships with the people around us and deepen our existing relationships with the natural world. We see ourselves more clearly and our world more compassionately. We take what we need and give back what we are able.

In this way, we advance the potential of our experience and the value of our presence here on earth. We justify the enormous investment the earth and its people have made in our lives and our potential. We become an integral part of the creative process through which everything flourishes.

THE ARC OF your own unique and irreducible existence extends from today to the eventual end of your journey on planet Earth. This ongoing synthesis of necessity and possibility belongs to you and no one else. It bears within it an array of possibilities that have yet to be realized.

How long will the arc of your existence continue? Some people die young, while others live for more than a century. Your time on earth could continue only for a few moments longer, but it may continue for a very long time. No one knows—and certainly not you. There are no guarantees. This realization introduces a note of urgency into the question of how you should live today.

Today could mark a beginning for you—a new opportunity to meet life's most pressing existential challenge: to maximize the value of each moment of your life. It's a chance to take a step along the way to becoming the kind of person you could become, to creating the kind of future for yourself and our world that you

could help create. A life of gratitude embraces each moment as a singular opportunity to create value—to advance the potential of the relationships that make life possible and sometimes, if we are fortunate, enable life to become wonderful.

Sometimes we create potential by what we give. Extending ourselves at work in order to make a deadline, collaborating with others to put on a play or clean up a park, joining a march to protest unfair laws or unjust treatment—these efforts help make life better for everyone.

At other times, we create potential by what we receive. Sitting quietly and listening to the burble of a stream, waiting with a friend in silence for news from the operating room, absorbing warm rays from the sun on a walk through a meadow or along a beach, these experiences can also maximize the value of a moment and a day. We feel deeply connected, both to the natural world that sustains us and to the people who support and nurture us. The way of gratitude calls us to cultivate the intensity of these relationships.

Again today, we have an opportunity to accept the necessities of the past and to engage the possibilities of the future. We can't do everything now, but we can do one thing—the one thing that will move us along the way of gratitude, if only by a step. As long as we fully embrace each moment, we are doing the one necessary thing.

Today is the first day of the rest of your life. No matter what has gone before, today presents you with a new and unique opportunity, one that has never come before and will never appear again. Make the most of it.

# ACKNOWLEDGMENTS

I WANT TO acknowledge a number of people who have been especially important companions to me in writing this book. For the past twenty-seven years, I've been engaged in an ongoing conversation about the challenges of developing a mature spirituality in the modern world with the members and friends of All Souls Unitarian Church in New York City. A large and progressive congregation, and one of the leading congregations in the Unitarian Universalist faith, All Souls celebrated its two hundredth anniversary last year. I'm deeply grateful to have been senior minister of the congregation for the past thirteen years.

I'm also deeply grateful to Laura Yorke, my book agent, whose amazingly tireless advocacy of this book and its importance enabled it to find a wonderful home at Random House. I'm grateful to Cindy Spiegel and Annie Chagnot, my editors at Random House, whose perceptive insights and steady guidance helped the book realize its promise. Others along the way provided significant editorial input as well, including Lari Bishop, Barbara Georgescu, Peter Georgescu, Nicole Kirk, and Elisabeth Robinson. In addition, countless more individuals—and you know who you are—provided the kind of emotional, spiritual, and logistical support that is essential to completing a book like this. To all of you, I offer my heartfelt gratitude. Thank you, thank you, thank you!

Most of all, I owe a debt of gratitude to my wife, Holly Atkinson, and my daughter, Zoë Guengerich, to whom I have dedicated this book. I love them both without measure, and their encouragement has been indispensable.

Zoë was less than two months old when I preached my first sermon at All Souls. I'm inordinately proud of the strong and accomplished young woman she has become, and I'm deeply grateful to be her father. Her presence and potential continually motivate me to do my utmost to work toward a better world, especially for women. Zoë, you're the best!

For more than twenty years, Holly has been my lover and best friend, as well as my first reader and my constant intellectual companion. I have learned much of what I know about myself, and especially about my feelings and emotions, through our interactions. I'm fond of quoting a remark by Alfred North Whitehead, who once said of his wife, Evelyn, "By myself I am only one more professor, but with Evelyn, I am first-rate." I know how he felt, and why. Thank you, my love.

ॐ

# APPENDIX A

## *Galen's Gratitude Goals*

1. Take personally the needs of the natural world.

2. Increase the quality of your relationships.

3. Bless the sources of life that sustain you.

4. Make the best of each moment.

5. Create more beauty wherever you are.

6. Maximize human dignity.

7. Advance the potential of the future.

## APPENDIX B

### *First Light Meditations*

Water does not resist. Water flows. When you plunge your hand into it, all you feel is a caress. Water is not a solid wall, it will not stop you. But water always goes where it wants to go, and nothing in the end can stand against it. Water is patient. Dripping water wears away a stone. Remember that, my child. Remember you are half water. If you can't go through an obstacle, go around it. Water does.

MARGARET ATWOOD, B. 1939

Whosoever wishes to know about the world must learn about it in its particular details. Knowledge is not intelligence. In searching for the truth, be ready for the unexpected; change alone is unchanging. The same road goes both up and down. The beginning of a circle is also its end. Not I, but the world says it: all is one. And yet everything comes in season.

HERACLITUS OF EPHESUS, 535–475 B.C.E.

When I care to be powerful—to use my strength in the service of my vision—then it becomes less and less important whether I am afraid.

AUDRE LORDE, 1934–1992

Why should we live in such a hurry and waste of life? We are determined to be starved before we are hungry. I wish to live deliberately, to front only the essential facts of life. I wish to learn what life has to teach, and not, when I come to die, discover that I have not lived. I do not wish to live what is not life, living is so dear, nor do I wish to practice resignation, unless it is quite necessary. I wish to live deep and suck out all the marrow of life. I want to cut a broad swath, to drive life into a corner and reduce it to its lowest terms. If it proves to be mean, then to get the whole and genuine meanness of it, and publish its meanness to the world. Or if it is sublime, to know it by experience, and to be able to give a true account of it.

HENRY DAVID THOREAU, 1817–1862

Let's start with a fundamental human problem, and I don't mean race or religion or origin. I mean fear. Fright, my young friend, may be the first serious enemy you have to face in our society. It's the most destructive emotional bogeyman there is. Cold feet, panic, depression, and violence are all symptoms of fear—when it's out of control. But this feeling, ironically, can also trigger courage, alertness, objectivity. You must learn not to try to rid yourself of this basic, human emotion but to manipulate it for your own advantage. You cannot surrender to fear, but you can use it as a kind of fuel. Once you learn to control fear—to make it work for you—it will become one of your best friends.

JOSÉ TORRES, 1936–2009

People say, what is the sense of our small effort? They cannot see that we must lay one brick at a time, take one step at a time. A pebble cast into a pond causes ripples that spread in all directions. Each one of our thoughts, words, and deeds is like that. No one has a right to sit down and feel hopeless. There is too much work to do.

DOROTHY DAY, 1897–1980

The temptation is always to reduce life to size. A bowl of cherries. A rat race. Amino acids. Even to call it a mystery smacks of reductionism. It is *the* mystery. As far as anybody seems to know, the vast majority of things in the universe do not have whatever life is. Sticks, stones, stars, space—they simply *are*. A few things *are* and are somehow aware of it. They have broken through into Something, or Something has broken through into them. Even a jellyfish, a butternut squash. They're in it with us. We're all in it together, or it in us. Life is *it*. Life is *with*.

FREDERICK BUECHNER, B. 1926

My successes are not my own. The way to them was prepared by others. The fruit of my labors is not my own: for I am preparing the way for the achievements of another. Nor are my failures my own. They may spring from the failure of another, but they are also compensated for by another's achievement. Therefore the meaning of my life is not to be looked for merely in the sum total of my achievements. It is seen only in the complete integration of my achievements and failures with the achievements and failures of my own generation, and society, and time.

THOMAS MERTON, 1915–1968

Those who profess to favor freedom, and yet deprecate agitation, are people who want crops without plowing up the ground. They want rain without thunder and lightning; they want the ocean without the awful roar of its waters. This struggle may be a moral one; or it may be both moral and physical; but it must be a struggle. Power concedes nothing without a demand; it never did and it never will. Find out what people will submit to, and you have found out the exact amount of injustice which will be imposed upon them. The limits of tyrants are prescribed by the endurance of those whom they oppress.

FREDERICK DOUGLASS, 1818–1895

Anyone can become angry—that is easy, but to be angry with the right person, to the right degree, at the

right time, for the right purpose, and in the right way—
that is not easy.

ARISTOTLE, 384–322 B.C.E.

When you open yourself to the continually changing, impermanent, dynamic nature of your own being and of reality, you increase your capacity to love and care about other people and your capacity to not be afraid. You're able to keep your eyes open, your heart open, and your mind open. And you notice when you get caught up in prejudice, bias, and aggression. You develop an enthusiasm for no longer watering those negative seeds, from now until the day you die. And, you begin to think of your life as offering endless opportunities to start to do things differently.

PEMA CHÖDRÖN, B. 1936

The humble spirit: I learn the meaning of the humble spirit from the earth. The earth takes into itself the rain, the heat of the sun, and it works with these gifts of life to bring the magic out of itself to be used for growth and sustenance of all living things. The earth is good because it takes what life gives, and within itself it uses its gifts to make life abound. It waits for fruition and gathers its fruit unto itself for more life and more growing. I shall learn of the earth the meaning of the humble spirit.

HOWARD THURMAN, 1899–1981

To save the mind from preying inwardly upon itself, it must be encouraged to some outward pursuit. There is no other way to elude apathy, or escape discontent; none other to guard the temper from that quarrel with itself, which ultimately ends in quarreling with all humankind.

FRANCES BURNEY, 1752–1840

This is the true nature of home—it is the place of peace: the shelter, not only from all injury, but from all terror, doubt, and division. In so far as it is not this, it is not home; so far as the anxieties of the outer life penetrate into it, it ceases to be a home. It is then only a part of the outer world which you have roofed over and lighted fire in. But so far as it is a sacred place, a vestal temple, a temple of the hearth . . . it is home.

JOHN RUSKIN, 1819–1900

You gain strength, courage and confidence by every experience in which you really stop to look fear in the face. You are able to say to yourself, "I have lived through this horror. I can take the next thing that comes along." You must do the thing you think you cannot do.

ELEANOR ROOSEVELT, 1884–1962

One of the great liabilities of history is that all too many people fail to remain awake through great periods of social change. Every society has its protectors of status quo and its fraternities of the indifferent who are notorious for sleeping through revolutions. Today, our very survival depends on our ability to stay awake, to adjust to new ideas, to remain vigilant and to face the challenge of change.

MARTIN LUTHER KING JR., 1929–1968

Putting things off is the biggest waste of life: it snatches away each day as it comes, and denies us the present by promising the future. The greatest obstacle to living is expectancy, which hangs upon tomorrow and loses today. You are arranging what lies in Fortune's control, and abandoning what lies in yours. What are you looking at? To what goal are you straining? The whole future lies in uncertainty: live immediately.

SENECA, 4 B.C.E.–65 C.E.

This is the reality we live: aspiring to be at our best, longing for and sometimes finding meaning and connection within ourselves and with that which is larger than ourselves, we are undone by messy bathrooms, traffic jams, and burnt toast. I am not interested in spirituality that cannot encompass my humanness. Because beneath the small daily trials are harder paradoxes, things the mind cannot reconcile but the heart must hold if we are to live fully: profound tiredness and radical hope; shattered beliefs and relentless faith; the seemingly contradictory longings for personal freedom and a deep commitment to others, for solitude and intimacy, for the ability to simply be with the world and the need to change what we know is not right about how we are living.

ORIAH MOUNTAIN DREAMER, B. 1954

The possible redemption from the predicament of irreversibility—of being unable to undo what one has done—is the faculty of forgiving. The remedy for unpredictability, for the chaotic uncertainty of the future, is contained in the faculty to make and keep promises. Both faculties depend upon plurality, on the presence and acting of others, for no one can forgive him- or herself and no one can be bound by a promise made only to the self alone.

HANNAH ARENDT, 1906–1975

We eventually learn that spirituality is not about leaving life's problems behind, but about continually confronting them with honesty and courage. It is about ending our feeling of separation from others by healing our relationships with parents, co-workers, and friends. It is about bringing heightened awareness and compassion to our family life, careers, and community service.

JIDDU KRISHNAMURTI, 1895–1986

I am done with great things and big plans, great institutions and big success. I am for those tiny, invisible, loving, human forces that work from individual to individual, creeping through the crannies of the world like so many rootlets, or like the capillary oozing of water, which, if given time, will rend the hardest monuments of pride.

WILLIAM JAMES, 1842–1910

The question concerning faith is not, Shall I be a person of faith? The proper question is, rather, Which faith is mine? Or better, Which faith should be mine? For, whether a person craves prestige, wealth, security, or amusement, whether a person lives for country, for science, for God, or for plunder, that person is demonstrating a faith, is showing that he or she puts confidence in something.

JAMES LUTHER ADAMS, 1901–1994

Most human beings take it totally for granted that I am "me," and that "me" is this body, this mind, this knowledge and sense about myself which so obviously feels separate from other people. The language in which we talk to ourselves and to each other inevitably implies separate "me's," and "you's" all the time. All of us talk "I" and "you" talk, we think it, write it, read it, and dream it with rarely any pause. There is incessant reinforcement of the sense of "I," "me," separate from others. Isolated. Insulated. Not understood. How is one to come upon the truth if separation is taken so much for granted, feels so common sense? The difficulty is not insurmountable. Wholeness, true being, is here all the time, like the sun behind the clouds. Daylight is here in spite of cloud cover.

TONI PACKER, 1927–2013

Persistence. Nothing in the world can take the place of persistence. Talent will not; nothing is more common than unsuccessful people with talent. Genius will not; unrewarded genius is almost a proverb. Education will not; the world is full of educated derelicts. Persistence and determination alone are omnipotent. The slogan "Press on!" has solved and always will solve the problems of the human race.

CALVIN COOLIDGE, 1872–1933

You cannot hope to build a better world without improving the individuals. To that end, each of us must work for our own improvement, and at the same time share a general responsibility for all humanity, our particular duty being to aid those to whom we think we can be most useful.

MARIE CURIE, 1867–1934

At every moment in every person's life there is work to be done, always work to be done, some of it small, some of it Great. The Great Work, in a sense, always has to do with healing the world, changing the world, and, as a necessary predicate to that, understanding the world. You rise every morning aware that you are called to this work. You won't live to see it finished. But if you can't hear it calling, you aren't listening hard enough. It's always calling, sometimes in a big voice, sometimes in a quiet voice.

TONY KUSHNER, B. 1956

Although the world is full of suffering, it is full also of the overcoming of it. My optimism, then, does not rest on the absence of evil, but on a glad belief in the preponderance of good and a willing effort always to cooperate with the good, that it may prevail.

HELEN KELLER, 1880–1968

I become more and more certain, as the years go by, that wherever friendship is destroyed, or homes are broken, or precious ties are severed, there is a failure of imagination. Someone is too intent on justifying himself, or herself, never venturing out to imagine the way things seem to the other person. Imagination is shut off and sympathy dies. If we know what it is that makes other people speak or act as they do, if we know it vividly by carefully imagining all that may lie behind it, we might not quarrel. We might understand. Often we could heal the wounds.

A. POWELL DAVIES, 1902–1957

What you see you become. What you see is a selective act of attention and interpretation. Although you are inundated by billions of bits of sensory impulses every moment, you selectively filter out the vast majority, allowing only a very small fraction into your awareness. What you allow into your awareness is determined by your habitual patterns of seeing and interpreting the world. . . . Your attention and interpretations create what you see and ultimately determine what you believe. A belief is simply an interpretation that you hold to be true.

DEEPAK CHOPRA, B. 1946

When you get in a tight place and everything goes against you till it seems as though you could not hold on a minute longer, never give up then, for that is just the time and the place the tide will turn.

HARRIET BEECHER STOWE, 1811–1896

A hundred times every day I remind myself that my inner and outer life are based on the labors of other people, living and dead, and that I must exert myself in order to give in the same measure as I have received and am still receiving. A human being is part of a whole, called by us the "Universe," a part limited in time and space. We experience ourselves, our thoughts and feelings, as something separated from the rest—a kind of optical delusion of our consciousness. This delusion is a kind of prison for us, restricting us to our personal desires and to affection for a few persons nearest us. Our task must be to free ourselves from this prison by widening our circles of compassion to embrace all living creatures and the whole of nature in its beauty. Only a life lived for others is worth living.

ALBERT EINSTEIN, 1879–1955

Oh, the comfort—the inexpressible comfort of feeling *safe* with a person—having neither to weigh thoughts nor measure words, but pouring them all right out, just as they are, chaff and grain together; certain that a faithful hand will take and sift them, keep what is worth keeping, and then with the breath of kindness blow the rest away.

DINAH MARIA MULOCK CRAIK, 1826–1887

Whether something lasts or not has nothing to do with whether it's made of stone or steel or wood or fabric. A house built all in wood can be a monument that lasts for hundreds of years because it seduces people to live in it, to use it and maintain it. Eternity depends on whether people are willing to take care of something. In Greece, ordinary white houses are repainted every year. Today we are often told to use materials and structures that are free of maintenance. But no building can be neglected entirely. We need constantly to renew our relationships—to the houses we live in, to our friends, to our own bodies—all the time, every day.

WERNER HERZOG, B. 1942

I invented this rule for myself to be applied to every decision I might have to make in the future. I would sort out all the arguments and see which belonged to fear and which to creativeness, and other things being equal I would make the decision which had the larger number of creative reasons on its side. I think it must be a rule something like this that makes jonquils and crocuses come pushing through cold mud.

KATHARINE BUTLER HATHAWAY, 1890–1942

Be selective about whom you take on as friends, colleagues, and neighbors. All of these people can have an effect on your destiny. The world is full of agreeable and talented folk. The key is to keep company only with people who uplift you, whose presence calls forth your best. But remember that our moral influence is a two-way street, and we should thus make sure by our own thoughts, words, and deeds to be a positive influence on those we deal with. The real test of personal excellence lies in the attention we give to the often neglected small details of our conduct. Make it your business to draw out the best in others by being an exemplar yourself.

EPICTETUS, 55–135

Work is love made visible. And if you cannot work with love but only with distaste, it is better that you should leave your work and sit at the gate of the temple and take alms of those who work with joy.

KAHLIL GIBRAN, 1883–1931

Do not think that love, in order to be genuine, has to be extraordinary. What we need is to love without getting tired. How does a lamp burn? Through the continuous input of small drops of oil. If the drops of oil run out, the light of the lamp will cease. What are these drops of oil in our lamps? They are the small things of daily life: faithfulness, punctuality, small words of kindness, a thought for others, our way of being silent, of looking, of speaking, and of acting. These are the true drops of love. Be faithful in small things because it is in them that your strength lies.

MOTHER TERESA, 1910–1997

Remember how long you have procrastinated, and how consistently you have failed to put to good use your suspended sentence from the gods. It is about time you realized the nature of the universe (of which you are part) and of the power that rules it (to which your part owes its existence). Your days are numbered. Use them to throw open the windows of your soul to the sun. If you do not, the sun will soon set, and you with it.

MARCUS AURELIUS, 121–180

Let no one think that the birth of humanity is to be felt without terror. The transformations that await us cost everything in the way of courage and sacrifice. Let no one be deluded that a knowledge of the path can substitute for putting one foot in front of the other.

MARY CAROLINE RICHARDS, 1916–1999

Hatred, which could destroy so much, never failed to destroy the one who hated, and this was an immutable law. . . . I imagine one of the reasons people cling to their hates so stubbornly is because they sense, once hate is gone, they will be forced to deal with pain.

JAMES BALDWIN, 1924–1987

Keep busy with survival. Imitate the trees. Learn to lose in order to recover, and remember nothing stays the same for long, not even pain. Sit it out. Let it all pass. Let it go.

MAY SARTON, 1912–1995

Nothing that is worth doing can be achieved in our lifetime; therefore we must be saved by hope. Nothing which is true or beautiful or good makes complete sense in any immediate context of history; therefore we must be saved by faith. Nothing we do, however virtuous, can be accomplished alone; therefore we are saved by love. No virtuous act is quite as virtuous from the standpoint of our friend or foe as it is from our standpoint. Therefore we must be saved by the final form of love, which is forgiveness.

REINHOLD NIEBUHR, 1892–1971

May I be no one's enemy, and may I be the friend of that which is eternal and abides. May I wish for every person's happiness and envy none. May I never rejoice in the ill fortune of one who has wronged me. May I, to the extent of my power, give needful help to all who are in want. May I never fail a friend. May I respect myself. May I always keep tame that which rages within me. May I accustom myself to be gentle and never be angry with others because of circumstances. May I know good people and follow in their footsteps.

EUSEBIUS, C. 263–339

I had learnt to seek intensity rather than happiness, not joys and prosperity but more of life, a concentrated sense of life, a strengthened feeling of existence, fullness and concentration of pulse, energy, growth, flowering, beyond the image of happiness or unhappiness.

NINA BERBEROVA, 1901–1993

Look at your life in the same way you'd look through an attic, deciding what you're going to keep, what you're going to throw out. You're moving from a house with a large attic but you've got only a small trailer to make the move. Some things have got to get thrown out so that you have space in the trailer for the things that really mean a lot to you. In other words, there are things you've got to give up in order to have the time for the things that really make a difference, that really do give substantial results.

THANISSARO BHIKKHU, B. 1949

How far you go in life depends on your being tender with the young, compassionate with the aged, sympathetic with the striving, and tolerant of the weak and the strong. Because someday in life you will have been all of these.

GEORGE WASHINGTON CARVER, 1864–1943

Life is not intended to be safe. A safe life has too small a name for a creature of eternity. Life at its noblest and highest has a hazard about it; it ponders tomorrow but does not know it; it sounds the depths of the ocean, but knows not the hazards of the bottom. Life at its best takes a chance on righteousness no matter the hazard, no matter the cost. Life, when answering to its true name, lifts on wings, feeling no invisible hands supporting it.

ETHEL WATERS, 1896–1977

Go placidly amid the noise and the haste, and remember what peace there may be in silence. As far as possible, without surrender, be on good terms with all persons. Speak your truth quietly and clearly; and listen to others, even to the dull and the ignorant; they too have their story. Avoid loud and aggressive persons; they are vexatious to the spirit. If you compare yourself with others, you may become vain or bitter, for always there will be greater and lesser persons than yourself. Enjoy your achievements as well as your plans.

MAX EHRMANN, 1872–1945

Love the animals, love the plants, love everything. If you love everything, you will perceive the divine mystery in things. Once you perceive it, you will begin to comprehend it better every day. And you will come at last to love the whole world with an all-embracing love.

FYODOR DOSTOYEVSKY, 1821–1881

Now is the accepted time, not tomorrow, not some more convenient season. It is today that our best work can be done and not some future day or future year. It is today that we fit ourselves for the greater usefulness of tomorrow. Today is the seed time, now are the hours of work, and tomorrow comes the harvest and the playtime.

W.E.B. DU BOIS, 1868–1963

The "Seven Social Sins": Knowledge without character. Science without humanity. Wealth without work. Commerce without morality. Politics without principles. Pleasure without conscience. Worship without self-sacrifice.

MAHATMA GANDHI, 1869–1948

We are to regard the mind, not as a piece of iron to be laid upon the anvil and hammered into any shape, nor as a block of marble in which we are to find the statue by removing the rubbish, nor as a receptacle into which knowledge may be poured; but as a flame that is to be fed, as an active being that must be strengthened to think and feel—to dare, to do, and to suffer.

MARK HOPKINS, 1802–1887

Do not be too timid and squeamish about your actions. All life is an experiment. The more experiments you make the better. What if they be a little coarse, and you may get your coat soiled or torn? What if you do fail, and get fairly rolled in the dirt once or twice? Up again; you shall never be so afraid of a tumble.

RALPH WALDO EMERSON, 1803–1882

Perhaps each of us has a starved place, and each of us knows deep down what we need to fill that place. To find the courage to trust and honor the search, to follow the voice that tells us what we need to do, even when it doesn't seem to make sense, is a worthy pursuit.

SUE BENDER, B. 1933

What happens is that we realize that we are but a speck of dust, a plaything of events outside our reach. Nevertheless, we may at the same time discover that we have a certain liberty, as long as we live. There is within each of us a modulation, an inner exaltation, which lifts us above dependence upon the gifts of events for our joy. Hence, our dependence upon events is not absolute; it is qualified by our spiritual freedom. Therefore, when we speak of resignation it is not sadness to which we refer, but the triumph of our will-to-live over whatever happens to us. And to become ourselves, to be spiritually alive, we must have passed beyond this point of resignation.

ALBERT SCHWEITZER, 1875–1965

## CREDITS

## ABOUT THE AUTHOR

GALEN GUENGERICH is senior minister of the Unitarian Church of All Souls, a historic congregation located on the Upper East Side of Manhattan. He graduated from Princeton Theological Seminary and earned a Ph.D. in theology from the University of Chicago. His sermon at All Souls on the Sunday after 9/11, "The Shaking of the Foundations," was selected as one of seven responses to 9/11, along with speeches by President Bush and Governor Pataki, for *Representative American Speeches 2001–2002*. He is the author of *God Revised: How Religion Must Evolve in a Scientific Age* and a member of the Council on Foreign Relations.

galenguengerich.com